THE
LONDON
WAY OF
DEATH

BRIAN PARSONS

Sutton Publishing Limited
Phoenix Mill · Thrupp · Stroud
Gloucestershire · GL5 2BU

First published 2001

Copyright © Brian Parsons, 2001

Cover photographs: Front: A funeral in Lynton Road, Bermondsey. *Back*: An unusual horse-drawn hearse in the grounds of Woolwich Garrison in the early twentieth century.
Title page photograph: The funeral procession of Dan Leno.

British Library Cataloguing in Publication Data
A catalogue record for this book is available from the British Library.

ISBN 0-7509-2359-6

Typeset in 10.5/13.5 Photina.
Typesetting and origination by Sutton Publishing Limited.
Printed and bound in England by J.H. Haynes & Co. Ltd, Sparkford.

An early nineteenth century funeral procession. (*Author's collection*)

Acknowledgements

I am grateful to the many people who have assisted in the compilation of this book. Particular thanks are extended to Barbara Prest, Paul Rowden, Brendan Meade and Anthony Driver of SCI Funerals Ltd for access to material in the F.W. Paine collection; Darryl Smith; Dr Tony Trowles, Librarian at Westminster Abbey; staff at London local studies libraries; Dr Ian Hussein of the City of London Cemetery and Crematorium; David Grainger and Keith and Andrew Leverton of Leverton Funeral Service; Barry Albin of F.A. Albin & Sons; John Harris of T. Cribb & Sons, Roger Gillman of J.E. Gillman & Sons and all the other funeral directors in the London area who have assisted. I should also like to thank Dave Salmon whose encyclopedic knowledge of funeral vehicles helped to identify a number of hearses. Particular thanks is extended to Pravin, Satish and Rashma Patel for their efficient reprographic service. Finally, I must thank Richard Syred and Anthony Caldicott for proof-reading and making helpful comments on the text.

CONTENTS

Firing the salute over a soldier's grave at Brompton Cemetery, *c.* 1900. (*Living London*)

Picture Post of 23 April 1949 featured an article about the funeral of Jim Lloyd, a greengrocer of Battersea. The photographs showed the horse-drawn procession to St Mary's, Battersea, followed by burial at Wandsworth Cemetery. The writer commented that in London there were only 'thirty horses which are regularly used for funerals. These undertakers have the monopoly of them and they find the expense so high that they are considering selling them in the next few months. When they do, the few features of London life that link the present with the past will have become one less, and the petrol-engine will have registered another triumph.' Today, it would appear that the tide had turned, with the increasing number of horse-drawn funerals. (*Hulton Getty*)

INTRODUCTION

In 'Burying London', a chapter of *Wonderful London* published in 1904, T.W. Wilkinson observed that 'The Angel of Death seems to be continuously hovering over London. While he may not visit a secluded village once in a year he spreads his wings over some of the myriad houses in the mighty city every six minutes, and bears away an immortal soul. . . . Death is a great, ever-present fact in the world's capital.' Although just under a century later the frequency has probably declined, it is one certainty that continues.

London has a rich social, cultural and religious heritage and nowhere is this more easily detected than in death and funeral rituals. The sight of the hearse moving through the streets on its way to a church, cemetery or crematorium is perhaps the most visible aspect of the funeral. Yet this final journey is only one part of a complex series of events which usually commences immediately after death (but in some cases just before death) and continues until after the funeral.

As the ultimate rite of passage, funerals remind us of our own mortality. They are often painful occasions; the more personal they are the less likely we want to recall them. However, we can learn a great deal about ourselves and our attitudes to death by the manner in which we treat our dead. It is these rituals and traditions which are the subject of the photographs included in this book. Lives are briefly recounted and scenes from the funeral depicted and described. While the ostentatious funerals that came to be a hallmark of the Victorian period have gradually disappeared, at the end of the twentieth century a rediscovery of funeral rites has occurred, giving rise to new expressions, such as DIY funerals, woodland burials and families 'doing their own thing'.

An almost indispensable participant in the funeral is the funeral director – the professional operating in a largely hidden industry to serve the needs of the bereaved. London is credited with having the first undertaker to establish a business in England; as the capital developed so too did the industry. When William Boyce commenced trading in the late seventeenth century his primary function was to provide the coffin, transportation and the necessary accoutrements. As the years have passed society's needs have changed and today funeral directors supply a comprehensive range of services that reflect current demands.

Writings on virtually every aspect of London can be located. None, however, can be traced which focuses exclusively on how the capital's dead have reached their resting place. In this volume are images of funerals that have brought the capital to a standstill (such as those of royalty) alongside others which have passed by unacknowledged. The mourning customs of different cultures and faiths are also discussed and some are illustrated. In addition, the operation and development of the funeral industry forms a significant part of this book. Photographs of the firms that have served the bereaved, their history, their vehicles and premises together with places of burial and cremation are included not only to reveal what is a neglected byway of our social and industrial heritage, but to serve as a record of those who have provided a vital service to the people – both living and dead – of London. The Frederick Paine photographs provide a unique insight into the development of a highly respected south-west London firm of funeral directors.

Death and funerals are emotionally charged occasions, so a certain sensitivity has been a key consideration during the research and compilation of this book. By their nature funerals possess both a public and private dimension. The intention of this book is to provide a visual and descriptive insight into funerals taking place in London. It is not intended to be voyeuristic or to intrude into what is unquestionably a traumatic and personal occasion; an apology is unreservedly extended if any of the images in this book cause offence. Funerals are an important expression of mourning; the love and respect felt for the deceased is obvious in many of the pictures. It was felt appropriate to omit certain types of funeral, such as those of children. In addition, while the scope of this book is to provide a comprehensive record by including cultural and religious diversity, the lack of accessible material has limited its inclusion.

The photographs in this book have been drawn from a wide variety of sources: private collections, postcards, local history archives, commercial photographic libraries, periodicals and funeral directors. Many are published for the first time. Each image has been carefully researched to provide background details. If any readers can add to the information or know of any photographs of London funerals that could be included in a further volume, the author would be glad to hear from them via the publisher. In many cases neither the death nor the subsequent burial or cremation will have taken place in the capital; this is particularly the case with royalty. All images date from between 1900 and the end of 1999, with the exception of Bernie Grant's funeral.

Every attempt at tracing the copyright holders of the photographs has been made. If an oversight has occurred, an apology is offered in advance and any corrections will be included in any subsequent editions of this book.

Brian Parsons
London
February 2001

1 *A Century of Change*

Disposal of the dead has always been and remains an important concern for any society. Historically, it has been a community-led event where many participate in the mainly religious funeral rituals that have been passed down through generations. However, while the community still participates, a key theme throughout the twentieth century has been the increasing separation – physically and metaphorically – of the living from the dead, resulting in a decline in the degree of involvement in funerals. Although the theme of this book is the past one hundred years, it is worth briefly reviewing several key developments in the nineteenth century – arguably the most influential period in respect of death and funerals – to consider their impact in the last century and to place the transition in context.

Victorian funerals were characterised by their extravagance and pretension. Charles Dickens referred to the 'fat atmosphere of funerals' and criticised the great expense and unnecessary pomp of the processions. *Oliver Twist*, *Great Expectations*, *Martin Chuzzlewit* and *Household Words* contain scathing descriptions of funerary expenditure frequently attributed to the aspirations of the middle classes. Not surprisingly, the nineteenth century undertaker also receives heavy criticism, examples being Mr Mould and the employees of Trabb & Co. in *Martin Chuzzlewit* and *Great Expectations* respectively. Writing in *The English Way of Death*, Julian Litten describes undertakers as 'In the main . . . a semi-educated band with neither trade nor union affiliation, and greedy – the occasional client was brought to financial ruin by undertakers charging over-inflated and extortionate prices for an unnecessary spectacle that few could afford or understand.' Much of the ritual and many of the accoutrements provided by the undertakers – the wands, the mutes and the hatchments – had been taken from their eighteenth-century forerunners – the Heralds and the College of Arms who were responsible for the funerals of the nobility. Others, such as the tray of feathers, were more recent. Detailed descriptions of their activities can be found in Julian Litten's book and also *Death, Burial and the Individual in Early Modern England* by Clare Gittings.

Mourning dress was an equally important industry. Crêpe – a fabric from eighteenth-century Italy – symbolised deep mourning and became synonymous with the textile firm Courtaulds which manufactured considerable quantities. It was particularly associated with the 'Widow of Windsor', Queen Victoria, following the death of her husband, Albert. Mourning warehouses flourished; at the height of their popularity there were four in Regent Street alone. Items made from jet – a kind of hard coal – were the official mourning jewellery, the best came from Whitby, Yorkshire. Other types were also available: French jet which was cut, black glass. Jewellery using the dead person's hair was also popular. Mourning etiquette, particularly for ladies, was important – withdrawal for a period of twelve months before resuming one's place in society was required. The absence of money made a funeral a doubly dreaded occasion. Paupers' funerals, or those paid for by the workhouse, carried a stigma and were to be feared. Burial would be in a common grave where others were already or where others would follow. The high levels of adult and infant mortality until very recently created a familiarity with death. Many deaths occurred at home and the body remained there until the time of the funeral.

Yet the nineteenth century witnessed a number of reforms in the disposal of the dead. Firstly, the Births and Deaths Registration Act of 1836 (revised in 1874) brought about a system for the formal recording and medical certification of death. Secondly, there was change to the place of burial. Historically, the Church of England had provided burial space. With the migration from the countryside to the towns and the demand placed on urban churchyards, many burial grounds had become overcrowded and unhygienic. Although a few cemeteries had opened to provide burial space for dissenters, such as Bunhill Fields near Old Street, this monopoly on burial provision continued until 1832 with the opening of London's first garden cemetery at Kensal Green by the General Cemetery Company. Its landscaped forty acres provided a secure and permanent resting place and the opportunity for expressive memorials. Further cemeteries were established by private companies until a *cordon sanitaire* was created around the centre of the city comprising Highgate, Kensal Green, Brompton, Norwood, Nunhead, Tower Hamlets and Abney Park. Following the Metropolitan Interment Act of 1850, which finally closed urban churchyards, these cemeteries, together with those opened by the burial boards in later years, served the needs of Londoners very well. Once occupying rural areas they have since become a feature of the urban landscape.

In 1852 the London Necropolis and National Mausoleum Company opened its vast cemetery at Brookwood in Surrey. Designed as an alternative to London cemeteries, the coffin and mourners travelled on one of the twice daily trains from the Necropolis station near Waterloo. Entries in the registers of central London funeral directors J.H. Kenyon detail the delivery of coffins to the Necropolis station in time for the morning train to Brookwood. However, many Londoners still preferred more local and accessible burial.

The last major development for nineteenth-century funerals was cremation. In 1885 the first cremation in Britain took place at Woking. A number of reformers, led by Sir Henry Thompson, Surgeon to Queen Victoria, had campaigned for this sanitary form of disposal of the dead, arguing that it would reduce funeral expenditure, spare mourners from weather and prevent premature burial. Also ashes could be kept in columbaria safe from vandalism. After finally overcoming the objections of the Home Office, a London woman – Edith Pickersgill – was cremated on 25 March 1885, at the Woking Crematorium, established by the Cremation Society of England. Although the number of cremations in the closing years of the nineteenth century was modest, crematoria opened in many parts of Britain. For a more detailed account nineteenth century funerals see *The Victorian Celebration of Death* by James Stevens Curl.

Funerals in the early twentieth century were carried out in much the same manner as in the previous century, although trappings like trays of feathers, disappeared and less elaborate hearses were introduced. However, when Queen Victoria died in January 1901 an immense funeral took place and similar scenes were recorded for Edward VII nine years later. Ordinary London funerals were still characterised by horse-drawn carriages, undertakers with wands, black clothes, streets lined with crowds, head-turning processions and an abundance of flowers. People generally died at home and the body rested there until the funeral. Occasionally, a coroner investigated the death, in which case the body would be held in a public mortuary for post mortem. The neighbourhood laying-out woman, who was often the local midwife as well, attended the house to wash and dress the body before the undertaker took measurements and returned with a finished coffin. Relations, friends and neighbours would then call to view the body and to express their condolences. On the day of the funeral the undertaker would return to the house and there would then be a procession to one of the seventy London cemeteries in existence by 1910.

The First World War saw a move away from elaborate funeral rituals. With so many men dying away from home there were no funerals to attend. Consequently, many traditions seemed inappropriate and gradually a reassessment of ritual occurred in the years following the war. Certainly this was the case for mourning wear. In *Mourning Dress: A Costume and Social History*, Lou Taylor comments:

> As the war continued the survivors had somehow to face up to the loss of almost a whole generation of young men and the creation of a new army – this one of widows and fatherless children. . . . Full ritual mourning dress seems not to have been worn down to the last detail. It was partly a question of morale, both for troops on leave from the trenches and the public at large remaining at home.

Correspondingly, Courtaulds had noted a marked decline in the sales of crêpe after 1912. In contrast, David Cannadine in *War and Death, Grief and Mourning in Modern Britain*, argues that the departure from Victorian mourning rituals can be attributed to a reduction in mortality, rather than the war. What is clear, however, is that following the end of the hostilities there was no return to pre-war rituals, instead new traditions and funeral procedures emerged. The unveiling of the Cenotaph (and indeed war memorials all over the country), the two minutes' silence on Armistice Day and the funeral of the Unknown Warrior expressed the collective grief of the nation. The immediate post-war years were also marked, at an individual level, by an increasing interest in spiritualism which presented the bereaved with an opportunity to contact the dead; the movement owed much to the influence of its greatest propagandist – Sir Arthur Conan Doyle. The 1920s and 1930s witnessed a number of important social changes. Improvements in public health, diet, medical facilities and income led to an increase in life expectancy and a decline in the mortality rate. In addition, the number of deaths in hospitals increased and as a result of new housing, such as the estates of blocks of flats built by the London County Council, fewer coffins rested at home.

The Second World War had a very different impact from the first on both a personal and a national level. While the number of deaths in the armed forces was considerably fewer, the civilian toll was much higher owing to air raids. It was not until after the war that the most noticeable changes in funeral rituals was seen; the growing preference for cremation, could be identified. In 1920 only 0.3 per cent of recorded deaths in England and Wales resulted in cremation at the eighteen crematoria in operation, three of which were in London. While this figure had only risen to 3.7 per cent in 1939, a number of London authorities such as Croydon, Islington and Enfield established crematoria. The Cremation Society of Great Britain encouraged cremation with the motto 'Save the land for the living' and its publication *Pharos*. Although they ran below full capacity in their first decade, after 1945 they were well able to cope with the new increased demand. In the 1950s further facilities opened in the London area, bringing the total to twenty-four. The last was built in 1974 to replace the 1904 City of London Crematorium. From 1950 to 1997 the national cremation rate increased from 15.9 per cent to 72.16 per cent, with 1967 being the first year when cremations outnumbered burials. Peter Jupp identifies a number of 'triggers' for this shift in his pamphlet *From Dust to Ashes*: the familiarity of mass and violent deaths during both wars; the erosion of neighbourhoods resulting in less need for funerals to be a display; economic advantage for local authorities, as land could be used for housing not cemeteries; and a change in attitudes by the clergy. Also, attitudes to death changed as life expectancy increased, religious belief declined and more people died in hospitals.

It was this change in the place of death – literally the separation of the living from the dead – which has unquestionably had the most impact on funeral ritual. In 1955, the anthropologist Geoffrey Gorer wrote a highly influential article arguing that death was now taboo, in much the same way that sex had been in the Victorian period. Death was viewed as dirty and shameful, something to be tidied away and controlled. Instead, have become voyeurs – images of death are commonplace in the media. This 'pornography of death', enables us to view the subject at arms-length and, therefore, to deny its reality. Although Gorer has been criticised for over-generalising, he was writing at a time when death was no longer an everyday experience and was becoming something that happened to the elderly.

Funerals in London between 1945 and the 1970s possessed all the hallmarks of this change in attitudes. The decline in religion led to many funerals taking place exclusively in crematoria and an ageing population increasingly dying in residential care meant that there was less likely to be an appropriate and significant place in the neighbourhood from which to start the cortège. Furthermore, the geographic mobility of family members and the increase in car ownership meant that many met the hearse at the crematorium; following the service the floral tributes would be examined before the assembled party went their separate ways if there was not a family home nearby for the wake. As burials declined one legacy remained: the rota minister. Until the 1980s, families opting for a Church of England service at a crematorium would find the service invariably performed by a duty clergyman. Up to seven or more services were performed on the same day, allowing no opportunity for pre-service contact or pastoral care. It was seen as a conveyor-belt system of half-hourly cremations; it was not surprising that funerals acquired an image of being impersonal and perfunctory. However, this was by no means the case across the board: communities maintaining a strong sense of tradition, such as those in parts of the East End and in areas near to the river in south-east London, maintain certain rituals. Floral displays, black clothing, lengthy processions, closed curtains and post-funeral gatherings could still be found.

A snapshot of funerals at the close of the twentieth century reveals a fascinating portrait of London life and the considerable change in funerals that has occurred over the last fifteen years. In general terms, the two distinctive areas of change must be the rediscovery of mourning rituals and the funerary expressions that represent the cultural mix of the capital. The most noticeable change is the return of the horse-drawn hearse. After an absence of only about thirty years an increasing number of funerals are now led by a pair or team of black horses. One of the most spectacular funerals in recent times took place in the East End following the death of Ronnie Kray in 1995. Although not illustrated here, an aerial photograph of his horse-drawn hearse and twenty-three limousines snaking their way over the Bow Flyover appeared on the front cover of a number of tabloids the following morning.

London has always had a multi-ethnic population and nowhere is this more evident than in the capital's cemeteries. The cultural diversity of areas such as Balham and Wood Green is reflected in the number of Poles and Greeks buried in Streatham Park and New Southgate cemeteries respectively. In the former, on the first Sunday in November families gather to pay their respects to the dead. The Jewish community has a number of cemeteries throughout London; funerals are managed through the synagogues which maintain traditions of simple ritual: a minimal interval between death and burial, the unadorned coffin and the stone-laying one year after burial.

The ethnic diversity of the capital has increased considerably since the 1950s and gradually cemeteries, crematoria and funeral directors have had to reconsider their services and adopt a more flexible approach to embrace the traditions of other religions. Today, visitors to South-West Middlesex or the City of London Crematoria will frequently observe Sikh or Hindu men carrying the coffin of a family member into the capacity-filled chapel. At the conclusion of the service the close family members will be led to the crematory to see the coffin enter the cremator. The funeral directors – in some cases from their own religious community – will return to the family's home or to a temple. Many municipal cemeteries now have an Islamic section with the graves facing towards Mecca. Following death the body will be prepared by the family and after a service in the mosque the coffin will be carried to the grave by the men. West Indian funerals often take place in a spirit of celebration. An important part of the ritual is seeing the deceased person and during the service in church an opportunity is provided for this. At the graveside members of the family backfill the grave to the accompaniment of hymns such as *The Old Rugged Cross* and *Amazing Grace*, and in a final act flowers are placed on and around the mound of earth before all return home for refreshments. Such a funeral may well occupy a large part of the day. Greeks will share a simple meal of cheese, bread and wine at the cemetery after the interment.

There can be no doubt that these rituals have contributed to a general reappraisal of funerals as families increasingly have a greater input in this last rite of passage.

Publications such as *Funerals and How to Improve Them*, *The Charter for the Bereaved* and the *Dead Citizen's Charter* have encouraged many to reconsider funerals. Also cemeteries, crematoria, funeral directors and ministers have faced new challenges. Do-it-yourself funerals are on the increase, when the family purchase a coffin and supply their own transport, and design and lead the funeral service in an effort to replace all paid professional helpers. Alternatively, a humanist officiant can be engaged to conduct the service. For those concerned with the environmental consequences of cremation, woodland burial is an alternative. One such burial ground is provided at the City of London Cemetery and another at the Natural Burial Area at East Sheen Cemetery. A number of firms supply wicker and cardboard coffins and some funeral directors have included them in their range. Music occupies an important place in funerals and many different forms and styles are increasingly being used, varying from a jazz band or piper leading the procession or playing at the graveside to soloists at crematoria and recorded secular music. At the funerals of many young men who died from AIDS-related diseases in the 1980s a pattern was established whereby families and friends would often devise an occasion to celebrate the life of the deceased. Funerals at the London Lighthouse have involved letting off balloons, releasing doves, personal tributes, secular readings, wreaths constructed of flowers from the families' gardens and those attending the funeral wearing particular colours.

More thought is also being given to the final resting place of cremated remains. Figures collated by the Cremation Society of Great Britain indicate a reduction in the number of remains being scattered in Gardens of Remembrance between 1970 and 1998 and an increase in those being removed from the crematoria. Options include burial in a family grave, placing in a columbarium and scattering at home, on a river, at sea or at a place favoured by the deceased.

As an alternative to the motor hearse, the coffin of a narrow-boat lover was gently transported on a barge along the Grand Union Canal to the side of Kensal Green Cemetery for the funeral. The key element here is that funerals belong to the bereaved. Funeral directors are optional facilitators – although it is perhaps understandable that most families feel they could not perform all the tasks provided by them – while cemeteries and crematoria provide a largely indispensable service. However, it is the need to 'get it over with' and the perceived risk of doing things differently which inhibits creativity at funerals. The Natural Death Centre in north-west London – publisher of the *Natural Death Handbook* – provides information on all aspects of self-managed funerals, including back-garden burial, burial at sea, alternatives to coffins and a list of funeral directors who can provide as much or as little assistance as required. The funeral of Diana, Princess of Wales, which took place in full public view and with much participation from friends and family, has shown a wider audience that funerals need not conform to a predetermined ritual. (Those wishing to read further on the aspects of death in this country over the centuries should consult *Death in England: An Illustrated History*.)

The following pages cannot totally represent every dimension of the funeral ritual. As will be seen, the majority of images show funerals that took place in the first half of the twentieth century. Any researcher compiling a similar volume in 100 years time would, no doubt, produce a very different survey.

2 *Royal Funerals*

Four reigning monarchs died during the twentieth century. Since Queen Victoria in 1901 their funerals have tended to keep to an established tradition and used London only en route to the place of burial at Windsor. For the three kings, Londoners have had an opportunity to pay their respects during the lying-in-state at Westminster Hall, in addition to witnessing an impressive procession to Paddington station. All have required considerable preparation and unsuspecting visitors to The Mall and Whitehall at 4.30 am a few days before the funerals would have witnessed an eerie rehearsal.

Queen Victoria's death at Osborne House, on 22 January 1901, brought to a close a reign of almost sixty-four years. Her coffin was taken across The Solent on the Royal Yacht *Alberta* to Portsmouth and by train to Victoria station. The procession then made its way from Buckingham Palace Road to The Mall, then towards St James's Street, through Piccadilly, Hyde Park, Marble Arch, Edgware Road, Praed Street and, finally, to Paddington station. At Windsor station the horses, having an unusually heavy load, kicked away and broke the traces from the gun-carriage. Prince Louis of Battenberg suggested using a naval guard of honour to drag the gun-carriage and a new tradition was born, as later pictures show. After the service in St George's Chapel the coffin rested in the crypt before interment in the mausoleum at Frogmore, where Victoria was placed in the sarcophagus next to Albert.

The horses misbehaving at Windsor. (*Illustrated London News*, 6 February 1901)

Queen Victoria's lying-in-state at Osborne House watched over by the Queen's Company Grenadier Guards. (*Daily Graphic*, 24 January 1901)

The procession to Paddington at St James's. Just before the procession left Victoria station a mounted soldier galloped out of the station to a point where, when waving his flag, he could be seen by the next look-out. (*Daily Graphic*, 4 February 1901)

The procession at Wellington Arch: a view from St George's Hospital, now the Lanesborough Hotel. The bearer party comprised officers of the Foot Guards and the Household Cavalry. (*Daily Graphic*, 9 February 1901)

The scene at Paddington station. (*Daily Graphic*, 4 February 1901)

George, Duke of Cambridge died on 17 March 1904. In a funeral 'marked by a wealth of military pomp and circumstance, inviting comparison to that . . . of the Duke of Wellington', the last surviving grandson of George III and Commander in Chief of the British Army 1856–95, was taken from Westminster Abbey to be placed in a mausoleum in Kensal Green Cemetery beside his wife Louisa, who had died in 1890. Watched over by a detachment of Grenadier Guards, the coffin rested overnight in St Faith's Chapel before it was placed under the lantern in front of the High Altar, prior to the service. *Left*: the Grenadier Guards bearing the coffin from Gloucester House, Piccadilly, on the evening before the funeral. (*Daily Graphic*, 23 March 1904)

The King (Edward VII) and the Prince of Wales following the coffin down the nave of Westminster Abbey. (*Daily Graphic*, 23 March 1904)

The gun carriage passing Marlborough House on its way to Kensal Green Cemetery. (*Illustrated London News*, 26 March 1904)

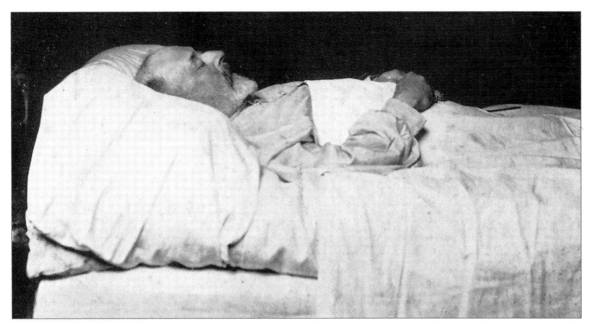

Edward VII died at Buckingham Palace on 6 May 1910 and lay in state in the purple-hung Throne Room for the following eleven days, then his coffin was then taken to St Stephen's Hall, Westminster. Over the following three days in excess of a quarter of a million people filed past. His funeral on Friday 20 May was modelled on Queen Victoria's, except there were more troops; many were still fighting in South Africa at the time of his mother's death. The international procession had five bands and finished with a detachment from the Police and Fire Brigade. In St George's Chapel, Windsor, the coffin was placed on a catafalque which descended slowly after the singing of the National Anthem. (*Author's collection*)

Lying-in-state in the Throne Room at Buckingham Palace. (*Author's collection*)

Transferring the coffin to Westminster Hall on 17 May 1910. (*Author's collection*)

The family around the coffin in Westminster Hall. (*Daily Graphic*, 18 May 1910)

The procession to Paddington station at Marble Arch. (*Author's collection*)

A view of Edward VII's gun carriage. (*Author's collection*)

The archbishop receiving the coffin at St George's Chapel, Windsor.

George V died on 20 January 1936 at Sandringham. His coffin was watched over by gamekeepers and gardeners in the estate church before being taken by train from Wolferton to Kings Cross. At the station the Imperial Crown was fixed to the coffin. In the procession through London King Edward VIII noticed a bright object 'dancing along the pavement' – The Maltese Cross had fallen from the crown, but it was duly retrieved. At Westminster Hall the coffin was covered with a pall from Westminster Abbey first used for the funeral of the Unknown Warrior in 1920. Over four days nearly one million people filed past the coffin. (*Author's collection*)

George V's coffin on the gun carriage. (*Author's collection*)

The final view of the coffin before the catafalque descended. (*Author's collection*)

The flowers at
Windsor Castle.
(*Author's collection*)

George VI died at Sandringham on 6 February 1952. After lying in state in Sandringham Church his coffin was brought to Westminster Hall. Four officers of the Household Brigade stood at each upper corner of the dais, while four Yeomen of the Guard were at a lower level. As with previous royal funerals, the gun carriage conveying the coffin was drawn by 150 sailors. Immense crowds lined the streets as the procession made its way to Paddington, where the Great Western locomotive *Eastnor Castle* conveyed the mourners while the coffin and bearers travelled behind in the *Windsor Castle*.

This photograph shows crowds queuing at night over Lambeth Bridge. Those on the north side of the bridge are walking in the snow flurries towards St Thomas's Hospital where they doubled back past Lambeth Palace before crossing Lambeth Bridge finally to head towards Westminster Hall. A total of 306,806 people passed through the hall during the three days. (*Illustrated London News Picture Library*)

The gun carriage passing through the gate at Marble Arch before turning into Edgware Road en route to Paddington. (*Illustrated London News Picture Library*)

Great-grandson of Queen Victoria, Admiral of the Fleet Earl Mountbatten of Burma, was killed at Classiebawn on the west coast of Ireland on the August Bank Holiday in 1979 when a bomb planted on his motor cruiser exploded. Mountbatten had planned his funeral arrangements himself. A day before the funeral, the coffin was brought from Romsey Abbey to the Queen's Chapel of St James's. The following morning the coffin was taken by gun carriage, drawn by 131 sailors with his horse, Dolly, immediately in front to Westminster Abbey where the hymns 'Jerusalem', 'I vow to thee, my country' and 'Eternal Father' were sung during the service. He was buried in the Broadlands Chapel at Romsey Abbey. Here the gun carriage is shown outside the Chapel Royal at St James's. (*Hulton Getty*)

The death of Diana, Princess of Wales, on 31 August 1997, shocked the world. The interval between her death and the funeral gave rise to an unprecedented outpouring of grief, the laying of thousands of flowers outside Buckingham and Kensington Palaces and other venues and the signing of countless books of condolence. Her funeral service at Westminster Abbey was watched by millions worldwide. For many, the most poignant sight was the throwing of flowers by onlookers as the hearse made its way through the streets of north London to the M1. The photograph shows the hearse just before it reached Althorp House, where she was buried. (*PA Photos*)

3 The Place of Burial and Cremation

There are over 140 cemeteries in the London area today, varying in size from a few acres to over 200. In *London Cemeteries: An Illustrated Guide and Gazetteer*, Hugh Meller estimates that their collective acreage is around 3,000, 'about the size of one of London's smaller boroughs'. While places like Highgate, Nunhead, Brompton, Kensal Green and Brookwood met nineteenth-century demands, the expansion of the suburbs and the increasing pressure on the existing burial space in the following century saw local authorities and a few private companies open new burial grounds. North Sheen and the adjacent Hammersmith New Cemetery opened in 1926 at Chalker's Corner (named after a firm of funeral directors – since closed – at the nearby crossroads), as existing space at Fulham Palace Road and Margravine Road had been exhausted. Others at Alperton (1927), Gunnersbury (1929), Pinner (1933), Grove Park (1935) and Paddington Mill Hill (1937) indicate the responsibilities of municipal authorities. However, few cemeteries have opened since the 1940s.

As already mentioned, prior to 1902 Londoners desiring cremation were taken to Woking. The opening of Golders Green Crematorium in that year, when the percentage of cremations in England and Wales was only 0.07 per cent, was followed by a number of facilities in the London area, despite the fact that by 1950 just under 16 per cent of cremations were recorded. The City of London (1902), Norwood (1915), Hendon (1922), South London (1936), St Marylebone (1937) and Mortlake (1939) were followed by numerous post-war crematoria, starting with Kingston (1952), South-West Middlesex (1954) and Lambeth (1958). Finally, in 1967 the number of cremations exceeded that of burial. There are now twenty-four crematoria in the London area handling a yearly average of just over 46,000 cremations. Nationally, around 72 per cent of deaths are followed by cremation.

For those who were offered Westminster Abbey as the final place of rest, cremation preceded interment. At first the small casket of cremated remains was carried to the grave. However, in the mid-1920s the Sacrist Dr Jocelyn Perkins arranged for the casket to be placed in a full-size coffin during the service. At the moment of committal a small door in the corner of the coffin was opened and the casket discreetly interred.

Despite the current high preference for cremation, space is still required for burial and its provision is an increasing area of concern as cemeteries become full and new ground becomes increasingly difficult to locate. The London Boroughs of Hackney and Tower Hamlets have no new burial space and the cemeteries opened by other local authorities in the 1920s and 1930s, as extensions to their nineteenth-century predecessors, are rapidly being filled. Some authorities have provided new sites some distance from their borough boundaries, such as the London Borough of Islington's Trent Park Cemetery at Cockfosters or adjacent allotment sites or recreational ground as have been used at Chiswick New and Camberwell New cemeteries. At Wandsworth Cemetery an 8 ft mound has been carefully created over old burial ground to provide new graves.

The ethnic diversity of London has meant that cemeteries now provide Muslim sections with the graves facing east towards Mecca, such as at Hatton, opened by the Borough of Hounslow in 1974, although Brookwood continues to be a favoured resting place. The Jewish community has long had a tradition of providing their own burial grounds with over fifteen in the London area, including new sites such as Edgwarebury which opened in 1976.

Since the end of the Second World War many private cemetery companies have fared badly. In the 1950s some companies such as East London, Beckenham, Manor Park and New Southgate have survived by converting their cemetery chapels into crematoria in an attempt to generate new revenue from the increasing preference for cremation. Other cemeteries, with a declining number of new grave spaces and increasing maintenance costs, simply closed. By the late 1970s the Abney Park Cemetery Company that owned Abney Park, Chingford Mount, Greenford Park and Hendon cemeteries had all been acquired by the local authorities. Similarly, Nunhead cemetery was acquired by the London Borough of Southwark in 1975 from the successors to the London Cemetery Company, although its more notable northerly sister – Highgate – was rescued by a private company on behalf of a group of 'friends'. However, the first nineteenth-century London cemetery, Kensal Green and the West London Crematorium, opened in 1939, continue to flourish under their original owner, the General Cemetery Company.

The London Necropolis Company Railway ran a daily service to Brookwood until the Westminster Bridge Road premises was partially damaged in an air raid in April 1941. The service was never resumed, although the company had a London office at neighbouring premises until the 1970s. In 1917 a military section was opened at the cemetery under the supervision of the Commonwealth War Graves Commission. War casualties from many Allied nations are buried there and in 1958 the Queen unveiled the Brookwood Memorial – a magnificent rotunda of Portland stone commemorating those with no known graves. On 11 May 1950 the Bishop of Guildford dedicated part of the cemetery as the Glades of Remembrance for the burial or scattering of cremated remains. The London Necropolis Company was acquired by the Great Southern Group in 1972; the cemetery was subsequently sold, but it remains in private hands. Over 240,000 burials have taken place since its opening in November 1854. Today, among the foliage of mature Wellingtonias, evergreens and rhododendrons it continues to function as an operational cemetery.

A coffin prior to being loaded into a hearse van at the London Necropolis station, 121 Westminster Bridge Road, *c.* 1902, with the family waiting to board the train. The service ran until April 1941. (*Living London*)

The memorial to Robert Lowe, First Viscount Sherbrooke (1811–92), Brookwood Cemetery. A former MP for Kidderminster, Calne and London University, he was also Chancellor of the Exchequer and Home Secretary. This card was issued by the London Necropolis Company in November 1906 to notify their change of address from 2 Lancaster Place, Strand to 10 George Street, Hanover Square. (*Author's collection*)

The chapels at the entrance to Highgate Cemetery, *c.* 1920. The most famous of all the London cemeteries is arguably Highgate. Founded in 1839, it occupies a total of thirty-seven acres on the east and west sides of Swains Lane. It was certainly a popular resting place; by 1975 166,000 bodies had been buried in 51,000 graves. Karl Marx, Michael Faraday, George Eliot and Radclyffe Hall are buried there. The fortunes of Highgate's private owners (and its sister Nunhead Cemetery) declined after the Second World War; following its closure in 1975 it has been maintained by a group of 'friends'. The chapel has now been restored. (*Author's collection*)

Streatham Park Cemetery and South London Crematorium. This was one of the few cemeteries to be opened in the first decade of the twentieth century. Established on about 100 acres between Mitcham and Streatham by the Great Southern Cemetery, Crematorium and Land Co. Ltd, the first burial was on 14 January 1909. The crematorium was opened in 1936 and an adjacent chapel built by the Variety Artists' Benevolent Fund was dedicated in 1958. In the late 1990s the crematorium was completely refurbished. The photograph shows the Anglican chapel (now offices) in the 1930s. (*Author's collection*)

Battersea New Cemetery. Opened in 1891 to provide seventy acres of burial space for residents of the Borough of Battersea, the now mature poplars either side of the approach to the chapels remind one of an avenue in northern France. In 1958 the left-hand chapel (below) was converted into the North East Surrey Crematorium. The crematory now occupies the two *porte cochères* and the rear area of the spire. The Garden of Remembrance is situated on the right of the main drive. The entrance gates are shown above, the rear of the chapels in the 1930s below. (*Author's collection*)

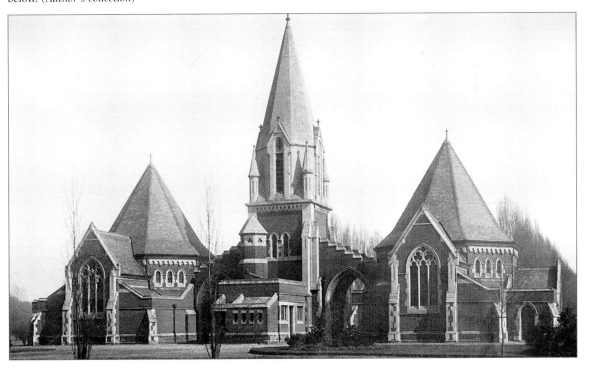

Camberwell New Cemetery was described by Sir Nikolaus Pevsner in *The Buildings of England: London 2: South* as 'quite impressively neo-gothic'. The foundation stone for these two large chapels, designed by Sir Aston Webb RA & Son, was laid in October 1928. Occupying a hillside site, the cemetery was intended to provide new burial space as the old cemetery, in nearby Forest Hill Road, which had served the Borough of Camberwell since 1856, was nearly full. In March 1939 the Honor Oak Crematorium was opened adjacent to the cemetery. (*Author's collection*)

St Marylebone Crematorium. Opened in 1937, to the designs of Sir Edwin Cooper RA (who also designed Marylebone Town Hall and the Port of London Authority building), the brick built Italianate style complex consists of the chapel to seat 175, cloisters, a garden of rest and a columbarium. As with many pre-war crematoria the coffin rests on a catafalque during the service, before being committed through the doors into the crematory. Later crematoria have alternative methods of committal, such as the descending catafalque (Honor Oak and Kingston) or curtains (South-West Middlesex, Eltham, Lambeth and Norwood). (*Author's collection*)

West Norwood (South Metropolitan) Cemetery. This must be south London's most distinguished cemetery. It was opened in 1837 and is situated on the crown of the hill, affording splendid views of south London. The two cemetery chapels were built to designs by Sir William Tite. The Anglican chapel (pictured here) resembled King's College Chapel, Cambridge. The Nonconformist chapel was converted into a crematorium in 1915. Following war damage both were demolished, and a new crematorium opened in September 1956. West Norwood is the resting place of the builder Thomas Cubitt, the preacher Revd Charles Spurgeon, the sugar merchant Sir Henry Tate and the cookery author Mrs Isabella Beeton. (*Author's collection*)

Jewish Cemetery Hoop Lane. Opened in 1895, this cemetery of sixteen and a half acres has two distinct sections. To the right of the prayer hall are the graves of Sephardic Jews, marked by flat slabs in white and grey marble and occasionally black granite. To the left are the more elaborate graves of members of the West London Synagogue. (*Author's collection*)

Woking Crematorium. The location of the first crematorium in England at Woking was no accident. As permission to build a crematorium within the Great Northern (London) Cemetery was rejected by the Bishop of Rochester, in whose jurisdiction the cemetery lay, the London Necropolis Company, who already had a railway link with Brookwood Cemetery some two miles away, offered land to the Cremation Society to build a crematorium in the St John's district of Woking. The first cremation took place on 26 March 1885. At the time the site consisted of little more than a cremation furnace. The chapel and crematory were built in 1888. Since opening, more than 130,000 cremations have taken place at Woking. This photograph shows the crematory and chapel *c.* 1916. To the left is an area for the burial of ashes. The original coke fired 'Gorini Cremation furnace' is pictured below. (*Author's collection*)

Golders Green Crematorium. Designed by Sir Ernest George, Golders Green has the distinction of being the capital's first crematorium. Since opening in 1902 more than 290,000 cremations have been carried out, including many famous people – Ramsay MacDonald, Stanley Baldwin, H.G. Wells, Ivor Novello, Sybil Thorndike, Alexander Fleming and Ralph Vaughan Williams. It is reputed that the largest gathering for a funeral at Golders Green was in 1966 for Harry Pollitt, founder of the Communist Party of Great Britain. The photographs show the West Chapel against the rather rural character of Hoop Lane (above) and the 240 ft cloister, east chapel and columbarium seen from the perimeter of the Garden of Remembrance (below). (See also advert on page 97) (*Author's collection*)

Woolwich Cemetery. Standing prominently on a hillside on a former part of Plumstead Common and occupying just over thirty-two acres, the cemetery was opened in 1856. The lodge in the centre of the photograph was demolished in 1960 and the foliage has developed considerably since this picture was taken. (*Author's collection*)

Opposite: City of London Crematorium – old and new. Although the City of London Crematorium at Ilford was the second crematorium to be built in London, the Corporation of the City of London had the unique privilege of establishing both the first and last municipal crematorium to be opened in the last century in the London area. Standing in a cemetery of 170 acres, consistently maintained to a high standard, the single chapel crematorium was opened in 1902. By the early 1970s demand was so high that it was decided to build a new two chapel crematorium, which was opened in 1973 by the Lord Mayor of London and dedicated by the Bishop of Barking. In 1999, 4,146 cremations were carried out here. (*City of London Cemetery and Crematorium*)

London's first private cemetery was Kensal Green. Founded in 1832 by its current owners, the General Cemetery Company, it occupies some 77 acres alongside the Harrow Road and counts royalty among its inhabitants. In 1939 the West London Crematorium was built at the far end of the cemetery. Beneath the Anglican chapel (pictured here) are brick vaulted catacombs; a recently restored hydraulic catafalque lowers the coffins from the chapel above. (*Author's collection*)

The Albin Memorial Garden. Opened on 13 November 1999 by local MP Simon Hughes, the Albin Memorial Garden meets a local need by providing an accessible location for depositing cremated remains. Caskets can be placed behind tablets or retained in the Ashebarium – the first of its kind in the UK – or scattered on the grassed areas. (*Author's collection*)

4 *Funerals in London*

When the prolific composer Sir Arthur Sullivan died aged 58 on 22 November 1900 at Queen's Mansions, Victoria Street, his funeral instructions stipulated that he be embalmed then buried with his parents in Brompton Cemetery. These arrangements were under way when the Dean and Chapter of St Paul's Cathedral consented to burial in the crypt preceded by a service in the Chapel Royal, St James's – at the request of Queen Victoria. Immediately after the coffin was lowered, his hymn *Brother, thou art gone before us* was sung. The illustration shows the interment in St Paul's Cathedral. (*Daily Graphic*, 28 November 1900)

'The King's Jester and the King of Jesters', Dan Leno, was born in St Pancras, but lived in south London during his years of fame. When this music-hall and pantomime artist, billed as 'the funniest man on earth', died, thousands lined the street for his funeral on 8 November 1904 as the cortège made its way from Atkins Road, Clapham Park, down Balham High Road to Lambeth Cemetery, Blackshaw Road, Tooting. (*Author's collection*)

Who was in the coffin? That was the question that had fascinated many people and which eventually led to Dr Tristram, Chancellor of the Diocese of London, issuing a Faculty to permit the exhumation of Thomas Charles Druce's coffin on 30 December 1907 from Highgate Cemetery. The initial request had come from the widow of Thomas's son Mrs Annie Maria Druce, who believed that he had not died and that the coffin did not contain his body. She believed the body to be that of William John Cavendish Bentinck-Scott, Fifth Duke of Portland. She believed that tiring of his living as a London shopkeeper, Thomas Druce had staged his death as the most convenient way of shedding that identity. However, the exhumation proved the body to be that of Thomas Druce. Here the erection of a shed around and over the grave is shown in preparation for the exhumation. (*Daily Graphic* 25 December 1907)

Dr Thomas John Barnardo was born in Germany in 1845, and his name is still remembered today. Working in the East End during a cholera epidemic he procured a room in Stepney and started to teach 'rough, ragged boys of the district'. Homes were established in London, including the Girls' Village Home at Barkingside. Following his death on 19 September 1905 his coffin lay in state at the Edinburgh Castle Mission Hall in Limehouse. A lengthy procession, headed by the band of the Stepney Boys' Home, preceded the coffin to Liverpool Street station for the journey to Barkingside, where he was buried beside the Children's Church. *Left*: The service in the marquee at the Girl's Village Home. (*Daily Graphic*, 28 September 1905)

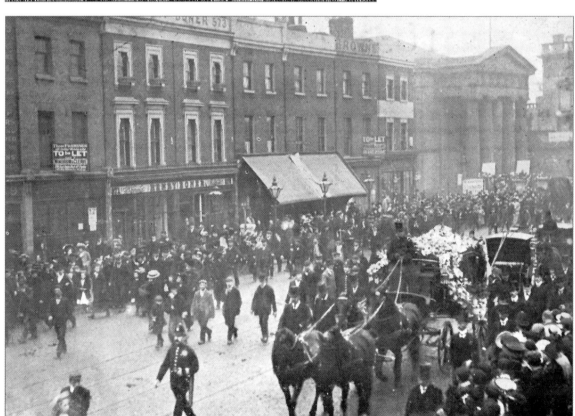

The funeral procession passing Stepney Causeway. (*Author's collection*)

At Barkingside station. (*Author's collection*)

The scene at the Edinburgh Castle in Limehouse.
It took its name from a pub in the East End.
(*Illustrated London News*, 30 September 1905)

Following cremation at Golders Green on 18 October 1905, the ashes of Sir Henry Irving were placed in a coffin which rested at 1 Stratton Street, Piccadilly – the home of Lady Burdett-Coutts, Sir Henry's longtime friend. A continuous stream of visitors silently filed past the coffin in a flower-filled room. The following evening the coffin was conveyed by hearse to Westminster Abbey. It rested in St Faith's Chapel, before being transferred to the nave the next day for the funeral service, after which the ashes were interred beside Garrick in Poets' Corner. An estimated £5,000 was spent on wreaths for Sir Henry's funeral. He was the first person to be cremated before burial in the abbey. *Above:* Sir Henry Irving lying in state at Stratton Street (*Daily Graphic*, 18 October 1905)

Flowers beside the grave. (*Copyright Dean and Chapter of Westminster*)

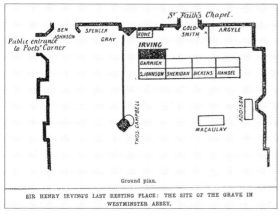

The site of the grave adjoining David Garrick's in Poets' Corner. (*Daily Graphic*, 18 October 1905)

On 13 July 1906 members of the Orpington, St Mary Cray and District Fire Brigade were travelling through Handcross in Sussex, on the way to Brighton, when the brakes on the Vanguard – a double-decker bus owned by the London Motor Omnibus Co. Ltd – failed and the bus crashed into a tree. Ten people were killed and over twenty-five seriously injured in what was Britain's first major road traffic accident involving a bus. Henry Hutchings, a part-time undertaker and fireman, was one of the victims and over 3,000 people attended his funeral. The inquest concluded that 'no-one was criminally responsible' for the accident. The photographs show the crowds gathering – probably in Lower Road, Orpington – and the funeral procession on its way to All Saints' Church. (*Author's collection*)

A railway funeral in Lynton Road, Bermondsey. Behind the wall, where the photographer is standing, is the Bricklayers' Arms goods yard. Featured in the banner at the end of the procession is a train, which probably indicates it is the funeral of a railway worker. (*Author's collection*)

After inheriting a considerable fortune from her grandfather – Thomas Coutts of the bank Coutts & Co. – Baroness Angela Burdett-Coutts was active in philanthropic works both in the East End of London and overseas. She founded Columbia Market (since demolished), the drinking fountain in Victoria Park was presented by her in 1862 and the nearby streets of Burdett Road and Coutts Road (since demolished) were renamed in her honour. Following her death aged ninety-two on 30 December 1906 at no. 1 Stratton Street, Piccadilly, nearly 30,000 people filed past her coffin before her burial in the nave at Westminster Abbey on 5 January 1907. The location was appropriate as she founded the nearby Great Peter Street Library and the church and school of St Stephen, Rochester Row, Westminster. *Above*: The hearse entering Dean's Yard Westminster (*Author's collection*)

Lying in state at Stratton Street (*Daily Graphic*, 4 Jan 1907)

The scene after the committal. (*Daily Graphic*, 3 January 1907)

Philanthropist and Chairman of the South Metropolitan Gas Company, Sir George Livesey's funeral on 17 October 1908 was one of the largest witnessed in south London. The coffin was brought from his home in Reigate and lay in state in the vestibule of the general office at the Old Kent Road gas works. A flag on the nearby gasometer hung at half mast. A one and a half mile long procession followed the coffin to Nunhead Cemetery where 500 men formed a guard of honour. Here it is seen in Asylum Road, Peckham; one of the company's gasometers is visible in the background. (*Author's collection*)

Following the death of His Highness the Maharajah of Cooch Behar (Sir Nripendra Narayan) on 18 September 1911, his coffin was brought by train from Bexhill to Victoria for cremation at Golders Green – there being no closer facility. Described as a 'first-rate shot, a keen shikari, an enthusiastic Turfite, a crack polo player, an adept at rackets and lawn tennis, and at indoor games, such as whist and billiards, hard to beat', the coffin, bearing a Union Jack, his helmet and sword, was met at the crossroads by Golders Green station by the 3rd Battalion of the Grenadier Guards and the 3rd Battalion of the Coldstream Guards. At the crematorium the service was translated into English. After cremation his ashes were sent to India for interment and a plaque was erected in the West Chapel at Golders Green. (*Author's collection*)

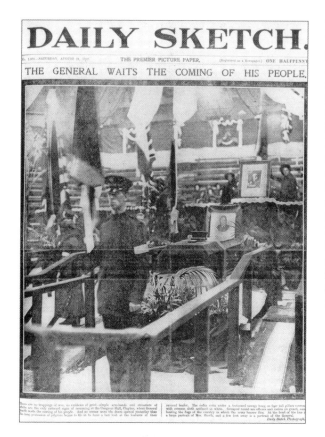

Following the death of General William Booth, founder of the Salvation Army, at Hadley Wood on 20 August 1912, his body was taken to lie in state at the Congress Hall, Clapton. On the evening preceding the funeral a service was held at Olympia, with an estimated 25,000 in attendance, before the coffin was finally transferred to the Queen Victoria Street Headquarters. 5,000 members of the army assembled on the Embankment to take part in the procession through the city to Abney Park Cemetery, Stoke Newington, where a two hour service was held. *Left*: Here the coffin is shown lying in state at the Congress Hall, Clapton. (*Daily Sketch* 24 August 1912)

The coffin surrounded by flags and palms passing Mansion House en route to Abney Park Cemetery. The procession took one hour to pass this point. (*Author's collection*)

Geoffrey William England, an airman attached to the Bristol Flying School at Lark Hill, Salisbury Plain, died on 5 March 1913 after the Bristol monoplane, with an 80hp Gnome engine destined for Rumania, fell from 600 ft while undergoing a duration test. The inquest held at Bulford Camp for the twenty-year-old heard that when the aeroplane was at between 4,000 and 5,000 ft the wind velocity increased from 20 to 35 mph, the left wing snapped off and, after rocking in the air, the aircraft dropped from the sky. The coroner recorded a verdict of accidental death. The funeral took place at Woking Crematorium on 12 March. (*Author's collection*)

Ivy Malyon was knocked down by a taxi on Tuesday 14 August 1917, aged thirteen. Taken to the Great Northern Hospital (now Royal Northern) in Upper Holloway with a fractured skull and other serious injuries, she died shortly after admission. Her funeral took place three days later. The commemorative postcard shows the procession passing Farbon & Co., the baker on Holloway Road, on its way to Islington Cemetery. (*Author's collection*)

'Incense in Kingsway' was the headline in the *Daily Sketch* describing Father Arthur Stanton's funeral procession. A faithful curate who ministered to the poor for over fifty years, his coffin, headed by a thurifer and churchwardens, was wheeled on a bier by fellow clergy from St Alban the Martyr, Brook Street, Holborn, to the Necropolis station at Waterloo. At 2.30 pm on 1 April 1913 a special train carried the coffin to Brookwood, where a crowd of over 1,000 had assembled for his interment in the church's own section of the cemetery. *Above*: His coffin being conveyed by fellow priests. (*Author's collection*) *Below*: The procession on Waterloo Bridge to the London Necropolis station in Westminster Bridge Road. (*Camden Local Studies and Archive Centre*)

Fr Arthur Stanton. (*Author's collection*)

Edith Cavell neither died nor was she buried in London. However, following her exhumation at the Tir National Cemetery in March 1919 – just over three years and five months after being executed in Brussels – Nurse Cavell's body was brought by train from Dover Marine station to Victoria and then by gun carriage, for a service at Westminster Abbey. Following a procession through the city, the coffin arrived at Liverpool Street station for the final journey to Norwich where she was buried with military honours at Life's Green in the shadow of the cathedral. Many postcards focused on her death, including images of her exhumed corpse. (*Author's collection*)

The removal from the Tir National Cemetery. (*Author's collection*)

The procession down Queen Victoria Street towards
Liverpool Street station. (*Author's collection*)

The memorial opposite the church of St Martin's-in-the-
Fields by Sir George Frampton RA, erected in 1920.
(*Author's collection*)

On 29 September 1916 an L31 bomb fell near Streatham Hill railway station. It exploded in the garden of Streatham Hill Modern School, killing four people on a London County Council tram waiting nearby. The conductor Charles Boys and the motorman John Gaymer, aged 31 and 45, died and a double funeral was held on 6 October.

Thousands lined the route to Streatham Cemetery, Garratt Lane, Tooting where the Revd John Darlington DD conducted the committal service. Wreaths were sent from staff at tramway depots all over London. The photographs show the funeral procession in Streatham. (*Author's collection*)

The funeral of a Yeoman of the Guard moving up Lambeth Road and then turning into St Mary's Church, Lambeth, adjacent to Lambeth Palace. Although the identity of the deceased is unknown, the date is around 1919. (*Author's collection*)

The funeral of the Unknown Warrior took place on 11 November 1920, following a suggestion by a young army chaplain, the Revd David Railton, to the Dean of Westminster Abbey, the Right Revd Herbert Ryle. A random selection was duly made from four unidentified bodies. On 10 November the journey began at Dover for London (using the same carriage that had conveyed Edith Cavell), before a full military funeral was held the following day. A full account of how the body was selected, the journey to England and the funeral appears in *The Story of the Unknown Warrior, 11 November 1920*, by Michael Gavaghan. *Right*: The coffin passing the Cenotaph after its unveiling. More than one million visitors attended and over 100,000 wreaths were laid in the first week. (*Author's collection*)

The grave in Westminster Abbey. (*Author's collection*)

'At 11.30 am on 17 August 1922 the great bell of Westminster Abbey began to toll,' reported *The Times*, '. . . and until the arrival of the funeral its solemn and melancholy impressive sound filled the crowded neighbourhood.' Just before twelve noon a hearse appeared in the densely crowded Parliament Square carrying newspaper proprietor Lord Northcliffe's flower covered coffin. After a service in the abbey and to the peal of muffled bells, the cortège – extending in length from the abbey to Victoria – made its way through streets lined four-deep in places for the seven mile journey to St Marylebone Cemetery at Finchley. As the procession passed, all traffic came to a standstill, while men removed their hats and women bowed their heads. Hundreds were assembled at the cemetery when the cortège arrived at 2.00 pm for the committal service, conducted for the 'chief' by the Bishop of Birmingham and the Vicar of St Jude-on-the-Hill, Hampstead. (*Copyright Dean and Chapter of Westminster*)

Succeeding Lloyd George as Prime Minister, Andrew Bonar Law's tenure lasted from 23 October 1922 to 21 May 1923. His death on 30 October the same year was followed by a cremation and burial of the ashes in Westminster Abbey on 5 November. The account of his funeral in *The Times* said: 'His life had not been spectacular. His burial in Westminster Abbey was not spectacular. Such pomp as was there to see was all ecclesiastical.' (*Copyright Dean and Chapter of Westminster*)

Founder of the Women's Social and Political Union, Emmeline Pankhurst, the suffragette leader, died on 14 June 1928, just a few weeks after British women over the age of 21 were granted full voting rights. Her funeral four days later was attended by thousands of women who lined the streets around St John the Evangelist, Smith Square, Westminster and Brompton Cemetery. Many were wearing the colours of the WSPU – purple, white and green. Four women stood guard overnight around the coffin which was covered with a purple pall. A further ten women acted as pall bearers. Although St John's escaped a bomb planted during the military suffragette campaign in March 1914, it was extensively damaged during air raids in 1941. (*Daily Sketch*, 18 June 1928)

The Right Revd Herbert Edward Ryle, the son of a former Bishop of Liverpool, died on 20 August 1925 aged 69. After an outstanding academic career at Cambridge, he became Bishop of Exeter in 1900, Winchester three years later and finally Dean of Westminster in 1911. At the abbey he led a successful campaign to raise funds for the fabric of the building. He was privately cremated, without ceremony, at Golders Green Crematorium, the day prior to his ashes being interred in the abbey, three feet from the grave of the Unknown Warrior. Johnson Street (off Horseferry Road) was renamed after him. The photograph shows the crowd around his grave. (*Copyright Dean and Chapter of Westminster*)

Publican for thirty-six years of the Railway Tavern, opposite the gates to West India Docks, and collector of antiques and curios reputedly worth £50,000, Charlie Brown – 'The Uncrowned King of Limehouse' – died on 5 June 1932. Born in Stepney, he welcomed visitors from all over the world, from sailors to the King of Spain. The Railway Tavern with (inset) Charlie Brown. (*Author's collection*)

Many local dignitaries attended his funeral on 9 June; hundreds lined the streets and shopkeepers put up black shutters as the cortège made its way to the City of London and Tower Hamlets Cemetery in Bow, where he was interred with his wife. *Right*: The hearse passing along Burdett Road by Pigott Street. (*Tower Hamlets Local History Library and Archives*)

The interior of the Railway Tavern with (inset) Charlie Brown as a young man. *(Author's collection)*

Some more of Charlie Brown's antiques and curios inside
the Railway Tavern. *(Author's collection)*

Following the death of author and traveller Rudyard Kipling on 18 January 1936, his coffin lay in state in the beautiful setting of the Middlesex Hospital Chapel. Designed by the eminent Victorian architect John Loughborough Pearson and completed by his son, the chapel's mosaic interior is a little known treasure of central London. Kipling was subsequently cremated at Golders Green and his ashes were interred in Poets' Corner, Westminster Abbey. (*Illustrated London News Picture Library*)

Fellow buskers, holding musical instruments, throw pennies – a symbol of their calling – into the grave of William 'Jock' McKeown at Streatham Park Cemetery in December 1938. He died on 2 December aged 73 years after being knocked down by a taxi. The funeral expenses were met by the companies appearing at the Strand and Gaiety Theatres whose queues 'Jock' had entertained for years. (*Hulton Getty*)

This long procession of two hearses (one probably used to convey floral tributes) and two flat-bed carts, also with flowers, is heading towards Central Hill, 1923. (*Author's collection*)

British individual speedway champion, Tom Farndon, died following a crash at the New Cross Speedway Stadium on 28 September 1935. A week later several thousand fans gathered at the stadium for a funeral service conducted by the Vicar of St James's Hatcham, the Revd J.B. Cowell, and attended by the Mayor of Deptford. The coffin – draped in the club's colours – was placed on trestles in the centre of the track; his helmet on top and the British Individual Championship cup on the ground. Burial took place in his native Coventry. (*Hulton Getty*)

This horse-led funeral took place in the Croydon area during the 1930s. (*Croydon Advertiser Group*)

Death in the course of duty often leads to colleagues' participation in the cortège. For those in the fire brigade the coffin is often conveyed on a fire tender. Although the year and location of this photograph are unknown it was probably taken in north London during the 1930s. (*Author's collection*)

Grandfather of the actress Angela Lansbury, member of the Labour Party for nearly fifty years, MP for the Bow and Bromley Division of Poplar since 1922 and one-time Mayor of Poplar, George Lansbury died on 7 May 1940 aged eighty-one. Many politicians, foreign dignitaries, clergy and local people packed St Mary's Church, Bow, for the service on 14 May 1940. *Above*: The cortège passing along Bow Road on its way to the City of London Crematorium. *Below*: George Lansbury's coffin being carried into St Mary's Church. (*Tower Hamlets Local History Library and Archives*)

Of long association with St Clement Danes – most importantly as Rector for thirty-one years – the Revd William Pennington-Bickford was instrumental in re-establishing the Danish origins of this historic church. The famous peal of ten bells was restored in 1919 and the first 'Oranges and Lemons' service instituted in March 1921. The church was destroyed following an incendiary raid on 10 May 1941. The Rector died five weeks later and his funeral was held on 23 June, in the church which then comprised no more than a tower and outside walls. On the busy Strand, with sunshine and hand-bell ringers pealing 'Oranges and Lemons', the coffin was guarded by Sea Scouts before cremation at Golders Green. St Clement Danes is now the RAF church. (*Hulton Getty*)

Brixton-born Labour peer, war-time inventor of the Morrison indoor table shelter, Mayor of Hackney and one-time Leader of the London County Council, Lord Morrison of Lambeth died on 6 March 1965. After cremation his ashes were scattered on the Thames from the fireboat *Firebrace* as it steamed slowly past County Hall following a memorial service at Westminster Abbey. (*London Metropolitan Archive*)

A full state funeral – an honour generally granted only to sovereigns – was deemed appropriate for Sir Winston Churchill in January 1965. After lying in state at Westminster Hall, he was taken by gun carriage for a service in St Paul's Cathedral. As he was piped aboard the *Havengore* at Tower Pier he was given a nineteen-gun salute. From Festival Pier his coffin was taken by motor hearse to Waterloo for the final journey, by train, to Hanborough and then to a private burial in the churchyard at Bladon. The photograph shows eight bearers at Festival Pier. (*London Metropolitan Archive*)

The death of His Eminence Cardinal Godfrey, seventh Archbishop of Westminster, took place on 22 January 1963. Born in Liverpool in 1889, formerly Rector of the English College in Rome and Archbishop of Liverpool, he succeeded Cardinal Griffin to the Westminster Diocese in 1956. Over 600 clergy attended his funeral at Westminster Cathedral on 29 January; interment in the Cathedral crypt followed the Requiem. (*Hulton Getty*)

Bernie Grant, Labour MP and former leader of Haringey Council, died on 8 April 2000. Born in British Guiana (now Guyana) in 1944, he came to Britain as a teacher in 1963, before quickly coming to prominence in local government where he achieved much for the local community. His open casket lay in state at Tottenham Green Leisure Centre before a funeral requested by Bernie Grant to be 'not too stuffy or churchy' at Alexandra Palace, attended by 3,000 people. (*Thabo Jaiyesimi/mckenzie heritage picture archive*)

It is customary at black funerals to view the deceased in the casket before burial. (*Jeni McKenzie/mckenzie heritage picture archive*)

At the cemetery the relatives and friends of the deceased backfill the grave. (*Jeni McKenzie/mckenzie heritage picture archive*)

Mourners placing flowers on the grave after it has been filled. (*Jeni McKenzie/mckenzie heritage picture archive*)

Consecration of memorial at the Jewish Cemetery, Plashet. A simple service is conducted by a rabbi who reads the inscription and offers up prayers in Hebrew, then English. (*Living London*)

Chinese graves in an east London cemetery early in the twentieth century. (*Living London*)

5 The Funeral Industry

Since the late seventeenth century undertakers have played a major part in laying to rest those who died in London. Indeed, the city is credited with having the first undertaker to open in business. William Boyce started trading in about 1675 in 'ye Grate Ould Bayley, near Newgate', followed closely by William Russell. Many undertakers provided the service as a sideline to their main craft such as cabinet making or upholstery.

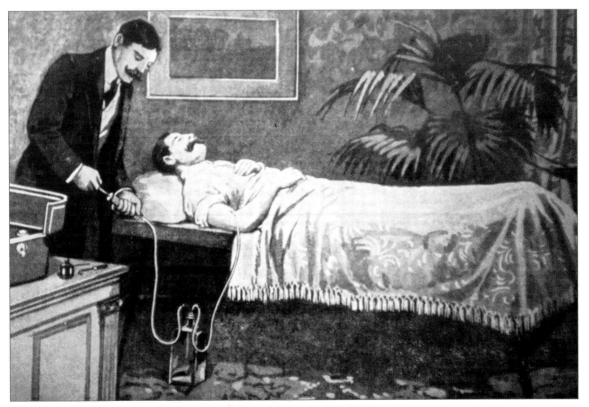

Although instruction in embalming was given to undertakers in London during classes held in August 1900, it was not practised to any great extent until they started to acquire custody of the body on their premises. However, as shown, the embalming could be carried out at home, as suggested by this advertisement of 1900. Today most firms in London carry out embalming on their own premises. (*Author's collection*)

The expansion of London from the late seventeenth century saw the development of the undertaking industry. A number of firms still in existence today are able to trace their roots back to the nineteenth century – a few even further. Perhaps the oldest firm still operating in London is Leverton of Camden. Founded in 1789 by John Leverton, it is currently run by eighth generation family members and trades from eight locations in north London. However, one important firm no longer in existence is Banting of St James's. William Westbrook Banting was the fourth generation to conduct royal funerals and those of the nobility. Instead of providing all the requirements for the funeral – the coffin, shroud, transport – he sub-contracted to other firms and simply directed the events. Following the deaths of both Queen Victoria and King Edward VII, Banting received instructions from the lord chamberlain for their funerals and contributed to the obsequies. On his retirement in 1928 the royal warrant was terminated. In later years J.H. Kenyon served the royal household and more recently Leverton's was used for the funeral of Diana, Princess of Wales.

A number of nineteenth-century firms still in existence and family owned are John Nodes of Ladbroke Grove, Mills (of circus fame) in Willesden, France's in Holborn and Walter Uden in south-east London. Some firms, such as William Stephen Bond, founded in Shepherd's Bush in 1869, Francis Chappell in Deptford started in 1840, J.H. Kenyon in central London and Ashton's in south London are now owned by large companies. Others, such as P.W. Ballard in Earl's Court, have closed or the name has been lost through merger, as is the case with the Marylebone firms of William Tookey – mentioned by Dickens in *Dombey & Son* – and Garstin, acquired by J.H. Kenyon.

The reputation of some nineteenth-century undertakers cast a dark shadow on the industry. In an effort to elevate their status, a trade association – the British Institute of Undertakers – was founded in the late 1890s. A later organisation, the British Undertakers' Association, founded in 1905, changed its name in 1935 to The National Association of Funeral Directors. In 1959 it introduced the Diploma in Funeral Directing and, in conjunction with the Office of Fair Trading, devised a Code of Practice in 1979.

In 1900 there were 360 entries for 'Undertakers' in *Kelly's Directory* for London, although the precise number of firms operating then is unknown. In 1927 the British Undertakers' Association estimated that there were at least 780 undertakers in business within a twenty mile radius of Charing Cross. The majority were one-man businesses, often carrying on another trade at the same time and usually carrying out only a modest number of funerals – perhaps fifty – each year. They did not possess their own stable, but would have hired horses from a carriagemaster who supplied a number of firms in an area. Henry Smith of Battersea Park Road served firms in south London, while Dottridge Brothers, on the City Road, operated predominantly north of the Thames. Larger firms such as W.S. Bond and J.H. Kenyon each had a fully equipped stable. A number of departmental stores also provided a funeral furnishing service: Army and Navy in Victoria, Harrods in

Knightsbridge and William Whiteley of Bayswater are examples. However, they usually sub-contracted the service to a neighbouring funeral firm. Harrods Funeral Service ceased trading in the 1980s.

In the 1930s the Co-operative Society started carrying out funerals in the north of England and then developed its business in London with societies such as London and South Suburban in south-east London and the Royal Arsenal and the London Co-operative in east London. Today the Co-ops retain a strong presence in these areas.

After the First World War many new firms sprang up and opened new branches, for example Francis Chappell in south-east London. The system which had been used in the nineteenth century by the carriagemasters was now extended to all aspects of the funeral director's work such as coffin preparation, removing and preparing the deceased and administration. Instead of each funeral office possessing costly vehicles, staff and facilities these could be located at and controlled from one central location and allocated to the branch when a client arranged a funeral. Staff at the head office would work on specific tasks such as embalming, coffin fitting and hearse driving, while branch offices would be run by a manager, who also conducted the funeral, and an assistant. Branches would consist of an office, where the funeral arrangements would be made, and one or two chapels of rest, where the deceased would be brought for viewing prior to the funeral. New branches could easily be integrated into this system, as could newly acquired firms. In the 1960s and 1970s both J.H. Kenyon and Dottridge Brothers purchased several existing firms in west and north London and started to run their operations from centralised locations. It is this change in ownership which is one of the most significant developments the industry has encountered in the twentieth century.

From the 1920s deaths increasingly occurred in hospital and undertakers provided chapels of rest, as bodies were less likely to be transported home to await the funeral. At first these were no more than converted rooms in the funeral director's premises, but in time they acquired a quasi-religious decor. In the 1930s a few firms had purpose-built premises with offices, viewing chapels and a service chapel, like T.H. Sanders at Richmond.

Although embalming techniques have been practised since the end of the last century when American 'professors' held classes in London, it was not until the 1950s, when funeral directors gained more custody of the deceased, that they actively promoted this relatively simple and inexpensive preserving treatment. One of the earliest notables to be embalmed was Sir Henry Irving, who died in Bradford. The *Undertakers' Journal* of November 1907 commented: 'The relatives and friends who saw the remains, including . . . Mr H.B. Irving, Mr Lawrence Irving and others, were all pleased with the result of the embalming, and marvelled at the perfect naturalness of the features, which had no more resemblance of death than though he had just dropped asleep.' Instead of embalming some undertakers used dry ice – frozen blocks of carbon dioxide – to arrest deterioration particularly when the coffin was kept at home. On the other hand, embalming at home was by no means unusual either. Embalming has become an increasingly important service with the tendency to take the body directly to the funeral director's premises, for viewings in the chapel and also with the increase in repatriation. In 1927 the foundation of the British Institute of Embalmers provided an opportunity to qualify for membership of a professional association, with many embalmers training at institutions such as the Lear School of Embalming. A similar organisation – the British Institute of Funeral Directors – exists for qualified funeral directors.

Coffins have changed substantially over the century. In the early years funeral directors would have made the solid wood coffins or purchased 'sets' for assembly from suppliers such as Dottridge Brothers or Ingalls, Parsons, Clive and Co. of Wealdstone. However, there was a steady decline in the use of hand-made coffins, which can be attributed to a combination of factors. Firstly, with the increasing preference for cremation, less substantial coffins were required. In a guide published in about 1904 by Dottridge Brothers, entitled *Cremation in London*, it stated that Golders Green Crematorium requested coffins of 'readily combustible wood, such as . . . Canadian Elm or thin Pine. English Elm is prohibited.'

Furthermore, the shortage of hardwoods and labour in the First World War, the increase in machine technology and the ravages of Dutch elm disease in the 1970s have all resulted in the introduction of mass-produced coffins constructed of chipboard. For many years it was commonplace to cover these coffins in black, violet or burgundy coloured cloth. More recently coffins have been available in medium density fibreboard. With concerns in the 1990s over emissions from crematoria, restrictions have been introduced, such as no painted or varnished coffins.

Despite these trends and the increasing awareness of ecological issues, today's trade journals still advertise hardwood coffins (albeit from sustainable sources), in addition to imported wood and metal 'American-style' caskets and the popular zinc-lined 'Last Supper' coffin which comes complete with a wood relief of the biblical scene on the side panels. At the other end of the range, cardboard or wicker coffins are by no means unusual. Likewise, coffin furnishings such as handles and nameplates, originally made of metal, were increasingly produced in wood and then more recently 'brassed' plastic or light metal. Nameplates are now computer-cut, instead of being produced on an engraving machine. Contrary to popular belief, fittings are never removed prior to cremation, nor is the coffin opened. The need to use pitch or wax to seal the joints of the coffin to prevent leakage has been eliminated by embalming and one-piece coffin liners which can be secured to the inside of the coffin.

Funeral directors' premises today show a move away from the austerity of yesteryear. Offices have tended to lose their gloomy, Victorian atmosphere: gone are the wood panelling, wine-red upholstered chairs, ferns and grandfather clock. However, F.W. Paine at Kingston, A. France in Conduit Street, Holborn, John Nodes in Ladbroke Grove, F. Upson & Sons on Tottenham High Road and the exteriors of

C.E. Hitchcock in Plaistow and Francis & C. Walters at Limehouse have still kept this distinguished appearance. 'Undertakers' parlours of such Victorian quality must be enjoyed before it is too late,' urged Geoffrey Fletcher in *The London Nobody Knows* from 1962. Although nearly forty years later the interior and window display at Walters have not lost their original furnishings and the exterior – particularly the sign – remains. Until the 1950s diamond-shaped hatchments could still be seen in some premises. Made of wood and bearing the family coat of arms, they would be carried in procession during heraldic funerals to announce that a death had occurred; after the funeral they would be hung as a memorial in the church where burial had taken place.

Generally premises are built or refurbished today to give a much softer and lighter décor. Pastel colours and less formal furniture, such as a sofa or dining table, can often be found in offices in place of a desk. Some firms also provide a coffin selection room. Windows, too, have tended to lose their displays of miniature coffins, urns and coffin handles, while scenes of activities such as coffin-making, at Henry Smith on Battersea Park Road, have long disappeared. Monumental masonry is often a feature; the variety of styles, materials and sizes ensures its presence even in the most modest shop fronts. More recently, the pre-paid funeral has become popular, ensuring future market share.

Traditionally, funeral directors have relied largely on reputation and loyalty for their custom. However, advertising in church magazines and local newspapers has always been a way of reinforcing their presence. The change in advertisements shows the developments within the industry. In the early part of the century motor vehicles and chapels of rest were included in advertisements, while today mention of the firm being family run or independently owned, with a twenty-four-hour service, a repatriation service, multi-lingual staff and pre-paid funeral plans can be found alongside an internet address. Once a male preserve, the industry now employs a considerable number of women, particularly in offices and increasingly in embalming and conducting funerals.

A number of new funeral directing firms have opened, particularly in the last twenty years, to serve particular social groups, such as the Indian Funeral Service, the African-Caribbean Funeral Service and Taslim Ali, specialising in Muslim funerals. The Jewish community has always provided a burial service through the synagogue with organisations such as Abrahams' Jewish Funeral Service supplying the coffin and other accoutrements. A number of cultures require the family or community members to prepare and dress the deceased prior to the funeral and funeral directors operating in areas such as Southall and the East End provide washing facilities. Other funeral directors provide specialist services, such as international repatriation and exhumation. Today there are about 450 funeral directors' offices listed in the Yellow Pages covering the London area. Very few in the area manage funerals as a sideline; the complexity of arrangements and level of demand essentially requires dedicated personnel to be available at all times.

A pioneer of embalming was George Stanley Lear. Born in Rochdale, Lancashire, in 1910 he became a Member of the British Institute of Embalmers before studying further in the United States. On arrival in London in 1935 he became the first freelance embalmer serving funeral directors, before forming a relationship with Ashton Brothers, funeral directors, at 369 Clapham Road, where in 1949 he established the Lear School of Embalming which he ran until his untimely death in May 1954. The Lear School of Mortuary Science continued until 1996; Lear Embalming Supplies continues to flourish. The illustration shows George Lear in about 1948. (*Author's collection*)

PRESERVATION

Post mortem preservation is of vital importance to all funeral directors. The Cardice method has inspired such confidence in the profession that its application and the satisfaction attendant thereon are becoming more and more widespread

CARDICE
definitely prevents decomposition

Write for full particulars to:

The Carbon Dioxide Co., Ltd.

Horseferry House, Westminster, London, S.W.1

Registered Trade Mark

DEPOTS THROUGHOUT
THE BRITISH ISLES

Telephone:
VICTORIA 8494

Telegrams:
"CARDIOX, SOWEST, LONDON"

When a coffin remained at home prior to the funeral, some funeral directors provided dry ice (frozen blocks of carbon dioxide) to prevent decomposition. (*Courtesy of Funeral Service Journal*)

Coffin finishing and french polishing in the premises of Muzzell in the early twentieth century. T.W. Muzzell was based at 7 Harrow Road and had served an apprenticeship with J.H. Kenyon. Note the large coffin nameplates on the bench to the right. (*Living London*)

The woodstack belonging to F.W. Paine in the 1930s. Elm boards would be stored then left to dry before use. The considerable quantity in store is indicative of the number of funerals the firm handled. (*F.W. Paine collection*)

A decorative letterheading showing the premises at Dorset Mews. (*Author's collection*)

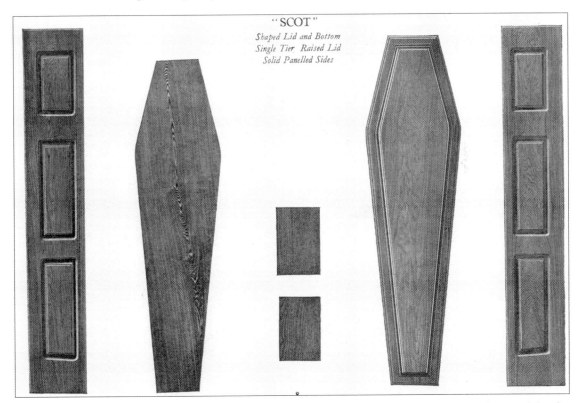

To minimise the labour-intensive activity of coffin making, 'sets' were available comprising the bottom, lid, sides and head and foot ends. The sides were ready kerfed and in this 'knocked down' condition the coffin could be easily assembled. This example was available in a variety of timbers from Dottridge Brothers in the early twentieth century. (*Author's collection*)

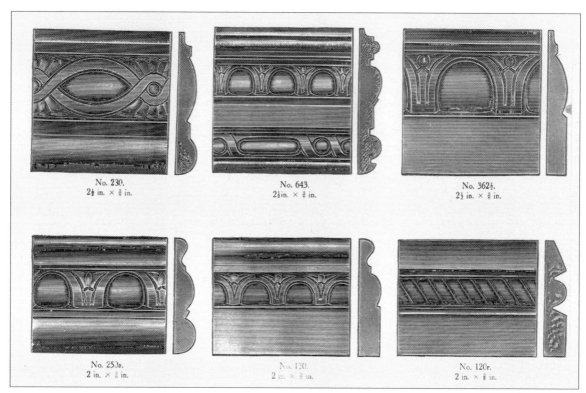

Decorative coffin mouldings. (*Author's collection*)

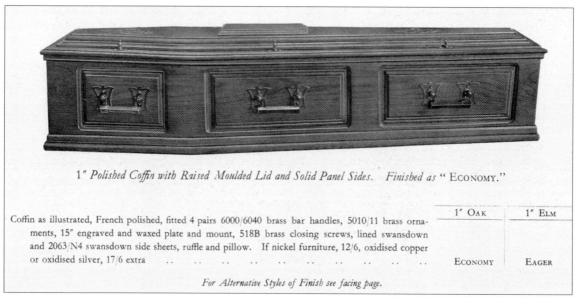

1" Polished Coffin with Raised Moulded Lid and Solid Panel Sides.   Finished as " ECONOMY."

	1" OAK	1" ELM
Coffin as illustrated, French polished, fitted 4 pairs 6000/6040 brass bar handles, 5010/11 brass ornaments, 15" engraved and waxed plate and mount, 518B brass closing screws, lined swansdown and 2063/N4 swansdown side sheets, ruffle and pillow. If nickel furniture, 12/6, oxidised copper or oxidised silver, 17/6 extra	ECONOMY	EAGER

For Alternative Styles of Finish see facing page.

A ready made coffin advertised in the Dottridge Brothers catalogue of 1933. In 1946 Dottridge introduced a wood veneer coffin using glues developed in aircraft manufacturing. (*Author's collection*)

Urns for cremated remains from the Dottridge Brothers catalogue of 1933. (*Author's collection*)

Automation increasingly assisted coffin production – this photograph shows a coffin being planed. (*F.W. Paine collection*)

A display of coffins, caskets, embalming equipment and funeral director requisites supplied by Dottridge Brothers, prepared for an exhibition in August 1947. (*Courtesy of Darryl Smith*)

Coffins under construction in the Dottridge workshop, probably in the 1930s. (*Author's collection*)

As an alternative to wood, hand-made wicker coffins are also available today. (*Courtesy of Somerset Willow Co.*)

A lightweight cardboard coffin suitable for burial or cremation. (*Courtesy of Compakta Ltd*)

In 1933 James Crook, funeral directors of 259 Kilburn High Road, opened their chapel known as 'Buckley Corner' – the premises occupy a site on the corner of Buckley Road and Kilburn High Road. It was dedicated by the Bishop of Willesden. The design was ecclesiastical, complete with stained glass, altar and *prie-dieu*, typical of its period. This chapel survived until the late 1990s. (*Author's collection*)

The firm of Henry Smith was founded in 1852 by Mr C. Smith of Chelsea, an important carriagemaster and supplier in the south London area. It was visited by the editor of *British Undertakers' Monthly* in May 1922 who noted that they possessed forty-five horses, twenty horse hearses, twenty carriages, twenty motor hearses and twenty motor landaulettes. A 60hp engine, driven by town gas, was used for kerfing the sides of coffins (to enable the shoulders to bend) to achieve the distinct shape. The firm has since moved to Garratt Lane, Earlsfield. Here premises at Battersea Park Road are shown in 1907. The 'behind the scenes' activities are clearly visible through the window. (*Author's collection*)

James Harold Kenyon came to London from Brighton and started trading at 12 Church Street, Kensington, having taken over the adjacent firm of Hunt in the late 1890s. As business expanded premises at Kilburn were purchased. Harold and Arnold – James's two sons – joined the company and a new head office at 45 Edgware Road was established. Sir Harold, as he became, was a member of Paddington and Kensington Councils and between 1932 and 1934 was simultaneously mayor for both boroughs. Kenyon's was responsible for assisting with royal funerals from the late 1920s to the 1980s. In the 1970s Kenyon International Emergency Service was formed to provide specialist repatriation services after disasters; many branches in north and west London were acquired around this time. (*Author's collection*)

The premises of Beckett & Sons at 152 Kentish Town Road around the time of opening in 1912 or 1913. The firm also traded from 70 Baker Street. The Kentish Town Road branch was closed in about 1920. *Kelly's Directory* for London lists the firm as 'Funeral Feathermen'. (*Author's collection*)

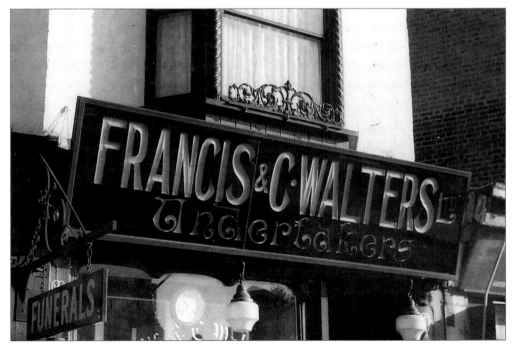

Although the family had connections with the undertaking trade since 1840, the Walter brothers, Francis and Chris, opened their office opposite Limehouse Church in 1902. Another office was in Stepney High Street, which was bombed during the Second World War. (*Author's collection*)

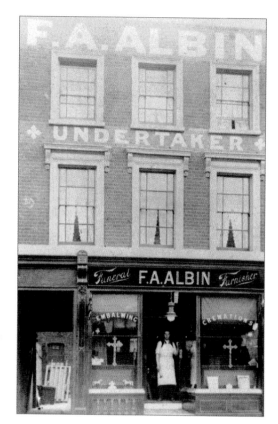

The premises of F.A. Albin at 62 Jamaica Road, Bermondsey, in the 1920s. The premises closed sometime in the 1970s when the head office moved to Culling Road, near Rotherhithe Tunnel. Today there are branches at Deptford and Mottingham. The Albin Memorial Garden, where cremated remains can be deposited, is situated between their Culling Road premises and Southwark Park. (*Courtesy of Barry Albin*)

T. Cribb & Sons was founded in 1881 by Thomas Cribb. After operating from premises in Rathbone Street, Canning Town, their new purpose-built head office was opened by Lord Young of Dartington on 30 November 1996 on 1.3 acres of land opposite Beckton Docklands Light Railway station. The complex comprises funeral arrangement and general offices, chapels of rest, coffin/casket selection room, mortuary, embalming room, coffin workshop and garage, with residential accommodation above. (*Courtesy of John Harris, T. Cribb & Sons*)

W. A. & J. R. HURRY,

Undertakers,

Funeral Carriage Proprietors,

And Monumental Masons,

132 THE GROVE,
53 CROWNFIELD ROAD,
STRATFORD, E.

➤ And 9 AXE STREET, BARKING, ➤

A Good Assortment of Wreaths and Crosses kept in Stock.

An undertaker's advertisement including the logo of the British Institute of Undertakers, which was formed as a trade association in 1898. In 1905 it was replaced by the British Undertakers' Association which changed its name in 1935 to the National Association of Funeral Directors. This advertisement appeared in the *West Ham Almanack* of 1900. (*Author's collection*)

TELEPHONE 139 WILLESDEN.

GEORGE BURCH.

FUNERAL FURNISHER & MONUMENTAL MASON

158, Manor Park Road and
134, High St., Harlesden, N.W. 10.

This splendid Arts and Crafts advertisement for George Burch, Funeral Directors of Harlesden, comes from a municipal guide dating from 1923. (*Author's collection*)

An advertisement from *Kelly's Directory* of 1930 showing the premises of S.E. Gregory, Chiswick. Note the diamond shaped hatchments hanging in both windows. (*Author's collection*)

66 *b* ADVERTISEMENTS.

Established 1896.

Phone: Chiswick **0758.** Telegrams: "Gregory, Undertaker, Chiswick."

S. E. GREGORY, M.B.U.A.
Funeral Director.

Funerals at lowest possible charges to suit all classes.
Cremations and Embalming. Sanitary Preservation.
:: :: Superior Motor Hearses and Landaulettes. :: ::
:: :: :: Improved Open Cars and Carriages. :: ::
:: :: :: Distance no object. :: :: ::

All Funerals personally   Private Mortuary
- - conducted. - -   - - Chapel. - -

CHIEF OFFICE:
2 **Devonshire Place, CHISWICK, W.4.**
Workshops & Garage: 2a Glebe Street, W.4

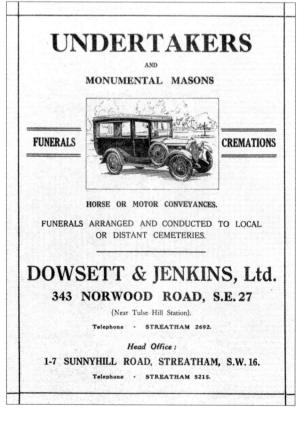

UNDERTAKERS
AND
MONUMENTAL MASONS

FUNERALS   **CREMATIONS**

HORSE OR MOTOR CONVEYANCES.

FUNERALS ARRANGED AND CONDUCTED TO LOCAL OR DISTANT CEMETERIES.

DOWSETT & JENKINS, Ltd.
343 NORWOOD ROAD, S.E. 27
(Near Tulse Hill Station).

Telephone - STREATHAM 2692.

Head Office:
1-7 SUNNYHILL ROAD, STREATHAM, S.W. 16.

Telephone - STREATHAM 5215.

An advertisement for the Streatham firm Dowsett & Jenkins, probably from the 1930s. (*Author's collection*)

Specially drawn for C.G. HATT & SON LTD. by HANSLIP FLETCHER

Occupying a prime site both at the time of foundation in 1871 and today was the firm of C.G. Hatt at 82 Kensington High Street, opposite Barkers. Like many firms it furnished both funerals and cremations, although in 1951, when this advertisement appeared, less than one fifth of deaths in Great Britain were followed by cremation. The founder, Charles George Hatt, died in September 1927 and his son George Charles three years later. At the time of closure in the 1960s the firm was part of the London Necropolis Company. Today the site is occupied by an optician. (*Author's collection*)

An early example of pricing transparency. In an effort to let the consumer make an informed choice, a number of firms displayed their scale of charges. This price tariff, published throughout 1900 in the parish magazine of St Mary Abbots, Kensington, provides detailed descriptions of the coffins, vehicles and other services offered by Mr Kenyon for each 'class' of funeral. Fees for the burial and clergy were extra. The appearance of such information today is rare. (*Author's collection*)

---

viii.   *S. Mary Abbots Parish Magazine.*

Mr. KENYON'S Residence, 12, CHURCH STREET, KENSINGTON.

Messrs. J. H. KENYON,
FUNERAL FURNISHERS.

ESTABLISHED 1830.   12, CHURCH ST., KENSINGTON,
Opposite S. Mary Abbots Church.

The RECORDS for the PAST 68 YEARS HAVE BEEN CAREFULLY KEPT

SCALE OF CHARGES FOR FUNERALS,
With the Speciality of Superior Carriages.

First Class Funeral.
A Funeral Car or Hearse, with four horses; three very superior Broughams, and pairs of horses; an inner shell lined with flannel, edged with rich white satin; a fine flannel and satin burial robe, or folding sheet; a stout oak outer case, French polished, with massive brass handles of appropriate design; an engraved brass inscription plate; 20 memorial service books; use of pall; attendance of conductor and the necessary assistants, £36.

Second Class Funeral.
A Funeral Car or Hearse, drawn by four horses; two very superior Broughams, with pairs of horses; an inner shell, lined with flannel; a stout elm outer case, French polished, with brass handles; an engraved brass inscription plate; memorial service books; use of pall; attendance of conductor and the necessary assistants, £22. Or with oak outer coffin, French polished, and finished with brass appointments, £26.

Third Class Funeral.
A Funeral Car or Hearse, drawn by pair of horses; two very superior Broughams, drawn by pairs of horses; an inner shell, lined with fine flannel; an oak outer coffin, French polished, with brass handles of an appropriate pattern,

and an engraved brass inscription plate; memorial service books; use of velvet pall; attendance of conductor and the necessary assistants, £21.

Fourth Class Funeral.
A Funeral Car or Hearse, drawn by pair of Horses; a very superior Brougham and pair of horses; an inner shell; an elm outer coffin, French polished, with brass appointments and inscription plate; use of pall, attendance of conductor and the necessary assistants, £12 12s. to £15 15s.

Fifth Class Funeral.
A Funeral Car or Hearse, with pair of horses; a very superior modern Carriage with pair of horses; a stout elm coffin, French polished, with brass handles; an engraved brass inscription plate; use of velvet pall, attendance of the conductor and the necessary attendants, £10 10s.; or with oak coffin, French polished, £12 12s.

INEXPENSIVE FUNERAL ARRANGEMENTS.
Hearse and pair, carriage and pair, a stout elm coffin, and every requisite £4, £5, £6, £7 10s., and £8 10s., according to the class of coffin required.

No EXTRA CHARGES UNLESS EXPRESSLY STIPULATED.
J. H. KENYON, LD.

ALSO,
45, Edgware Road, Marble Arch; 8, Harrow Road; and 35, Malvern Road, Kilburn.

MONUMENTAL SCULPTORS.

A coffin being carried from the house to the waiting hearse in Simms Road, Bermondsey, *c.* 1963. The funeral directors had brought the coffin to the house and encoffined the deceased after the funeral arrangements had been finalised. (*Courtesy of Barry Albin*)

An impressive fleet of Daimler vehicles used for the funeral of Mr Scolding, an assistant secretary of the former Royal Arsenal Co-operative Society.

The RACS merged with the Co-operative Wholesale Society in 1985 and their head office for the region remains at Woolwich. The RACS building is in the background, in Powis Street, Woolwich.
(*Both photographs courtesy of the Co-operative Funeral Service*)

'No more beautiful spot could be selected', said *The Times* about Brookwood Cemetery. The London Necropolis Company continued to encourage funeral directors to recommend Brookwood Cemetery, despite the closure of the rail service in 1941. The company traded from the adjacent premises at 123 Westminster Bridge Road until the 1970s. This advertisement appeared in the *Funeral Service Journal* in 1955. (*Courtesy of Funeral Service Journal*)

With only 0.07 per cent of funerals leading to cremations in Great Britain in 1900, advertisements promoting both the benefits of cremation and facilities like Golders Green could be found in publications and local guides of the period. The London Cremation Company continues to own Golders Green and Woking and more recently acquired St Marylebone Crematorium. This advertisement comes from *Marylebone and its Old Associations* issued by local estate agents in 1925. (*Author's collection*)

Frederick Paine is carrying his top hat as a coffin is carried from a cemetery chapel, probably in the 1930s. (*F.W. Paine collection*)

Derrick Leverton in front of a Rolls-Royce hearse in Hampstead in 1963 for the funeral of Hugh Gaitskell, the Leader of the Labour Party. (*Courtesy of Leverton & Sons*)

6 Funeral Vehicles

An important part of any funeral is the procession to the place of burial or cremation. The word 'funeral' is derived from the Latin 'funeralis' meaning a torch-lit procession. As many of the photographs in this book indicate, the cortège remains an impressive sight, especially with the return of the horse-drawn hearse.

The 1920s saw an increasing number of motor hearses on the streets, although it would be another thirty years before horses were replaced altogether; their absence, however, was only brief. The word hearse comes from the old French 'herse', meaning a 'harrow', a triangular implement with spikes attached, which came to be adapted for candlesticks and was used partly for light and partly for ceremonies. It became more and more magnificent, often being made of brass, with fringes and ornaments. By the seventeenth century it was used to bear the coffin from the home to the grave and by the late 1870s the glass-sided horse-drawn hearse began to appear, as the distance to the newly opened out-of-town cemeteries made shouldering the coffin or walking to funerals impractical. In country areas, however, the hand or wheel bier was still used for transporting the coffin, although it was still used in London at the funeral of Fr Stanton in 1913. Dottridge Brothers were able to supply both wheel biers and horse hearses. The horses used for hearses were generally Belgian Blacks. The British Undertakers' Association urged members to refrain from using black ostrich plumes from January 1914, as when the feathers became wet they were heavy, which put a strain on the horses' heads.

The early motor hearses were literally the coffin compartment of a horse hearse secured to the chassis. Trade journals carried advertisements for motor removal vehicles from about 1911 and for motor funeral vehicles in the following years. W.S. Bond and Henry Smith proudly advertised their new fleets in the trade journals published throughout 1915. The makes of funeral vehicles prevalent at any given time have largely reflected the domestic vehicles being produced. In the 1920s to 1940s Daimler, Austin, Wolseley, Leyland, Armstrong-Siddeley and Rolls-Royce chassis were being used for hearses and limousines; Humbers and Buicks were used in the 1950s and Fords in the 1970s. More recently Volvos, Mercedes and Citroëns have appeared. Some hearses could accommodate the coffin and up to four bearers; a dual-purpose hearse had a removable bier with replacement seats to turn it into a limousine. The Daimler DS 420 was generally held by the industry to be the classic funeral vehicle. Although production ceased in 1991, many are still in regular service. Alpe and Saunders at Kew Gardens, Coleman Milne and Woodall Nicholson have been the market leaders in specialist funeral coachwork. Black remains the predominant colour of funeral vehicles, although maroon, grey and midnight blue have been used over the last twenty years. White hearses for children's funerals are also available. To convey the deceased from the place of death to the mortuary a discreet van, often entitled 'private ambulance', is generally used, though an estate car is sometimes used as an alternative.

From the nineteenth century until the 1950s the rail network was used extensively for the routine transportation of coffins. Indeed, even as late as 1961 a coffin being loaded into a brake van at Waterloo station was included in the classic documentary *Terminus*. London has also been served by two rail links to cemeteries: the short-lived branch line to the Great Northern Cemetery at New Southgate served from Belle Isle station, just north of Kings Cross, and the London Necropolis Company line from Waterloo to Brookwood Cemetery. The increasing demand for horse-drawn hearses in recent years has seen at least two London firms – Cribb's at Beckton and F.A. Albin at Rotherhithe – acquiring their own horses and hearses. Despite the general use of motor vehicles, many funeral directors continue the tradition of walking or 'paging' the funeral as it moves away from the house and again on arrival at the church, cemetery or crematorium.

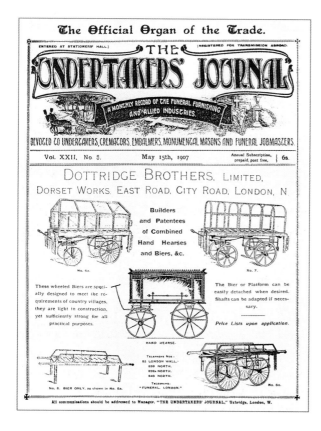

A Dottridge Brothers advertisement for the cover of *The Undertakers' Journal* of 1907, depicting their range of hand hearses and biers. (*Courtesy of Funeral Service Journal*)

This photograph of a coffin on a wheel bier was taken at a policeman's funeral. (*Author's collection*)

An unusual horse-drawn hearse in the grounds of Woolwich Garrison in the early years of the twentieth century. (*Greenwich Council, Greenwich Local History Library*)

A horse-drawn hearse belonging to F.W. Paine posing against the splendid backdrop of the Lion Gate outside Hampton Court Palace. (*F.W. Paine collection*)

A horse-drawn hearse about to depart for a funeral in west London during the 1920s. (*Author's collection*)

The Plaistow firm of C.E. Hitchcock was founded in July 1898 by Charles Edgar Hitchcock. This splendid horse-drawn hearse, with brass angels, probably dates from the early part of the twentieth century. (*Archives and Local Studies Library, London Borough of Newham*)

A horse-drawn hearse in east London. The absence of plumes indicates that the date was after 1916. Note the wands held by the undertakers beside the hearse. (*Author's collection*)

Ebbutt's Funeral Service can be traced back to 1718 when John Ebbutt, a carpenter and joiner, started in business in Orpington. In 1851 Ebbutt's Funeral Service was advertised in the *Croydon Directory* based at 20 High Street as builders, joiners and undertakers. In the 1880s the business was split: Charles Ebbutt & Sons became the monumental masons and H.D. Ebbutt & Sons the undertakers, with branches at Purley, Coulsdon, Selsdon and Wallington appearing throughout the twentieth century. In 1966 Ebbutt's joined Ashton Funerals Ltd to become Ashton Ebbutt Holdings. The business continues at 89 High Street, Croydon. (*Author's collection*)

T.H. Sanders' fleet at Preston Place, Richmond, comprising three hearses, four carriages and one enclosed carriage for removing the deceased from the place of death. (*F.W. Paine collection*)

F.W. Paine's Lancia hearse delivering a coffin, probably in the 1920s. (*F.W. Paine collection*)

Commencing business as undertakers and builders in about 1915, the firm of George Thomas Godfrey had premises at 7 Boundaries Road, Balham. Shortly before George's death in 1948 the funeral directing side of the business was split from the building side and his son Edward Alexander established an office at 7 Station Parade, Balham. In 1963 the neighbouring Tooting firm of J.E. Gillman acquired Godfrey's. E.A. Godfrey died in February 1989. The photograph shows the premises at Boundaries Road and their Commer hearse, probably in the 1920s. (*Courtesy of Roger Gillman*)

A 1916 removal vehicle owned by the south London firm A. & G. Ashton. Tracing its history back to 1840 when Ralph Ashton, a cabinet maker, founded R. Ashton Furnishing Undertakers, the company expanded under family ownership in the Kennington and Clapham areas. In 1946 the premises at 369 Clapham Road were acquired and served as the head office until closure in March 2000. In the early 1960s Jessica Mitford visited Mr Lawrence Ashton to discuss funeral procedures in England when writing her notorious book *The American Way of Death*. (*Courtesy of Funeral Service Journal*)

A flower decked Rolls-Royce Phantom hearse at a funeral in Walworth, *c.* 1950. H.W. (now J.W.) Simpson was situated in East Street, towards the end of the famous street market known locally as 'East Lane'. (*Author's collection*)

An impressive parade of Rolls-Royce hearses and limousines owned by T.H. Sanders of Richmond, probably in the 1930s. (*F.W. Paine collection*)

The wheel turns full circle as horse-drawn funerals reappear in London, such as this one seen after a funeral in East Sheen Cemetery in the early 1980s. (*Author's collection*)

A funeral using a Daimler fleet in Kennington, 1992. The Daimler DS 420 limousine and hearse were generally held to be the classic design for funeral vehicles by the industry. Production of the model ceased in 1991, although many continue in service. (*Author's collection*)

An adjustable bier inside a Rolls-Royce hearse constructed by J.C. Clark Ltd of Shepherd's Bush. (*Author's collection*)

Three hearses supplied by Dottridge Brothers. This Rolls-Royce dates from the 1940s.

An Austin Six.

An Austin. (*All three photographs courtesy of Darryl Smith*)

An advertisement for Alpe & Saunders, funeral coach builders. (*Courtesy of Funeral Service Journal*)

After initially hiring hearses and carriages from a carriagemaster, T.H. Sanders acquired premises at Preston Place, Richmond, to accommodate two hearses, two carriages and four horses. In 1934 a four year transition from horse to motor hearse commenced, with the purchase of Austin and Rolls-Royce vehicles. Over a five year period, starting in 1962, a fleet of Vanden Plas Princess hearses and limousines was purchased, including these seen at a funeral in Ham. (*F.W. Paine collection*)

An impressive Armstrong Siddeley cortège entering Streatham Park Cemetery, probably in the 1950s. Francis Chappell are the funeral directors. (*F.W. Paine collection*)

A funeral in Camden Town led by Ivor and Basil Leverton, probably in the 1960s. (*Courtesy of Leverton & Sons*)

Ford MkII Granada hearse and limousine, built by Coleman Milne and used by F.W. Paine in the 1970s. (*F.W. Paine collection*)

An operational Rolls-Royce hearse owned by F.A. Albin & Sons of Bermondsey. (*Courtesy of Barry Albin*)

7 The Frederick W. Paine Story

For many residents of south-west London the blue lantern is synonymous with Frederick Paine, Funeral Directors. Although some of the lanterns have disappeared and later branches had a clock instead, in locations such as Hampton Hill the lanterns are still a prominent local landmark.

Frederick William Paine, born on 4 April 1870 at Burritt Road, Norbiton, was the eldest of eleven children of Charles and Mary Paine. His father had founded a firm of house furnishers, estate agents and undertakers in 1884 and Frederick Paine, having traded in antiques in the Waterloo Road for a time, took over the family business at 8–9 Station Terrace, Coombe Road, New Malden. At the age of 24 Frederick Paine started to carry out funerals from tiny premises at Fountain Roundabout in New Malden – a move which infuriated the Kingston undertaking firm of Farebrother. Writing in an article in the *Surrey Comet* in May 1976, June Sampson recounts what happened next: 'Soon there was a clash of personalities. . . . The elegant, fastidious, self-aware Charles Walter Farebrother felt bitter antipathy toward the down-to-earth, plain speaking, supremely self-confident Mr Paine. Finally, Mr Farebrother rounded on Mr Paine and told him: "I can beat you in business any time I want so don't get too cock-sure." He then proceeded to open a rival establishment a few yards away from Mr Paine in New Malden. Mr Paine retaliated by opening in Kingston as near to Farebrother as he could.' That was in 1908. They continued to trade opposite one another at 24 and 21 London Road, Kingston, for the following ninety-two years, until Farebrother closed in July 2000. By this time both establishments were owned by the same firm. Research by Marian Hinton, Heritage Officer for the Royal Borough of Kingston, shows that in the early days of the business Frederick Paine had little capital and 'sometimes did not know from day to day whether he would have money to hire enough horses for the morrow's funeral'. However, the business developed considerably under his management and by 1917 he had established branches at Church Street, Twickenham and High Street, Teddington, in addition to the New Malden office. He possessed a large stud of horses and employed many staff. About the same time he acquired a motor hearse, the first in the district to do so. He was an advocate of embalming and attended embalming tuition in London in 1902.

The site at Kingston was impressive and occupied a large part of the Fairfield area. The head office remained at 24 London Road, while branches were supplied with coffins and vehicles which were housed at Westons Park. He also had a large monumental masonry department and the works, studio and showroom at 53 Eden Street, before moving to a considerable part of Fairfield West. In the centre of the studio was the chapel of rest, which was entered through an imposing arch with Doric columns. The masonry department later traded as Memorial Crafts Ltd. The inter-war years were a period of immense growth. In addition to opening branches at Raynes Park and Esher, Frederick Paine also established new offices in areas where the population was expanding, such as Tolworth, Worcester Park and Morden, the latter serving the 1930s St Helier Estate. Much thought was given to the external appearance and internal decoration of the branches. In addition to the blue lantern or clock, the entrance to some branches was flanked with columns of polished pink granite and the street doors were often inlaid with etched glass. Inside, the offices and chapels of rest were panelled in wood. Most branches also had a large display cabinet of brass coffin furnishings, such as at Twickenham, and stone memorials in the windows. A panel of frosted glass with a pink and yellow border and a blue scroll and star at the top was a feature of many chapels of rest. Where the chapel could not be accommodated inside the premises one was built at the rear, such as at Worcester Park and Sutton. Staff accommodation was generally provided above the premises. The furnishings and decoration of the branch at London Road would still be familiar to Frederick Paine.

The records of all the funerals that F.W. Paine ever carried out have been carefully preserved at the former head office. Each ledger contains much detail and a survey of nine decades of work indicates many changes in the range of coffins, services and costs. In addition, Frederick Paine's reputation led him to conduct funerals to many of the London cemeteries and home counties' churchyards, as people who had moved away continued to instruct the firm. In 1914 the cost of a No. 3 type elm coffin, horse-drawn hearse, conductor and bearers was £9 9s, plus burial fees and a minister. For a funeral with cremation at Golders Green the cost was £6 10s. A more elaborate burial, involving a lead coffin with an elm shell and solid brass handles followed by a journey to Highgate Cemetery cost £22 10s. In 1940 the cost of a violet cloth-covered elm coffin with simple ring handles, a motor hearse, removal of the deceased, conductor and bearers was £21, with a £6 10s 6d cremation fee at the South London Crematorium.

Although he had been ill for some time while living in Hove, Frederick Paine died suddenly on 20 March 1945 at London Road, aged 75 and was buried at Kingston, Cemetery. In announcing his death the *Surrey Comet* said that he was '. . . an omnivorous reader', an opera lover and a collector of bracket clocks and antique mugs. An active freemason, he was a member of six lodges. He was clearly a generous man and left legacies totalling £3,000 to his employees. He was not married and the business passed to his sister and co-director Mrs Ida Kate Moatt, who, together with her husband, continued to manage the firm. At this time the firm had thirteen branch offices. In his will Frederick Paine expressed the wish that the north London funeral wholesaling firm of Dottridge Brothers be given an opportunity to acquire the business. The trustees, however, rejected the bid and the business was eventually sold to the Alliance Property Holdings Ltd, which then, in turn, became part of the London Necropolis Company – owners of the vast Brookwood Cemetery and various funeral directing establishments in London and the home counties.

In 1962 the Fairfield site was demolished when the area around the cattle market was redeveloped. However, suitable accommodation for the vehicles, mortuary, coffin workshop and offices was found at Horace Road, about a quarter of a mile south of the centre of Kingston. This was named Bryson House after G. Bryson Richardson, one of the directors of the London Necropolis, and is from where the firm continues to operate. By this time further branches had opened at Chessington, Isleworth and Molesey.

Cornwall Property (Holdings) Ltd acquired the business in 1970 and two years later, crematoria owners the Great Southern Group (formerly the Great Southern Cemetery, Crematorium and Land Co. Ltd) took over. Frederick Paine had been a friend and contemporary of the founder of this firm, Frederick John Dyer Field, who had owned the funeral business of Messrs Bedford Sons and Slater in Farringdon Street and Blackfriars Road, founded in 1840. The company had opened Streatham Park Cemetery in 1907 and built the adjacent South London Crematorium in 1936. With the closure of Bedford and Slater around the time of the Second World War, the purchase of F.W. Paine marked the Field family's return to funeral directing. In 1977 they acquired Francis Chappell, another large London funeral firm with twenty-three branches, while continuing to increase their crematoria ownership. In 1982 Great Southern Group purchased Paine's long-standing rival Farebrother. Then in 1984 the company celebrated the centenary of F.W. Paine. To mark the occasion various events were held between November 1983 and the following April – orchestral concerts, a programme of salmon re-introduction to the Thames and the creation of a museum dedicated to the history of the firm at Horace Road. This includes photographs of branches, an original lantern, stained glass, hatchments, wands, miniature coffins used for client selection, handles and top hats. In 1994 the Texas-based organisation SCI – Service Corporation International – bought the Great Southern Group. Today there are twelve branches trading as Frederick W. Paine.

Throughout the twentieth century funeral directors' premises have changed to meet new demands. While the first chapels of rest appeared in the early years of the century, from the 1920s onwards some firms expanded by opening branches served from an operational centre. Here the scope of change, particularly in the premises owned by F.W. Paine in the Kingston-upon-Thames area, can be seen. *Above*: F.W. Paine letterheading from the 1930s. *Right*: F.W. Paine. (*F.W. Paine collection*)

The Norbiton branch at 29 Coombe Road in the 1930s. (*F.W. Paine collection*)

The Morden branch, forming part of the Crown Lane Parade. The branch was opened to serve the recently built St Helier Estate. (*F.W. Paine collection*)

Surbiton branch at 265 Ewell
Road prior to opening. (*F.W. Paine
collection*)

The Worcester Park office before relocation in the 1920s. (*F.W. Paine collection*)

The branch at 6 Coombe Lane, Raynes Park in the 1970s. Although owned by F.W. Paine, the masonry showroom on the right traded as Memorial Crafts Ltd. The lantern has since been removed and the description 'Undertaker' replaced by 'Funerals'. (*F.W. Paine collection*)

The exterior of the branch at 31/32 Church Street, Twickenham in the 1970s. In January 1975 the local press announced that the undertaking business of W.A. & W.R. Wake at 13 Church Street would be incorporated into Frederick Paine's neighbouring branch to become Wake and Paine. The Wake family had been in business as undertakers and builders for over a century. Thomas Alfred Wake, grandson of the founder, died on 26 August 1974. This photograph would have been taken shortly before a complete redecoration of the premises in Great Southern Group house style. (*F.W. Paine collection*)

The exterior of the Twickenham branch after refurbishment in January 1999. (*Author's collection*)

The former interior of the Twickenham branch. The six candlesticks would be placed around a coffin when it was taken home or to church. The display case of handles and crosses indicates the firm's range of alternative coffin furniture. The long photograph above the three candlesticks on the right is of Brookwood Cemetery. (*F.W. Paine collection*)

Twickenham: the interior. The long photograph just visible in the centre of the arrangement office in the right hand corner is of Brookwood Cemetery. The hatchments are similar to those in the museum at Horace Road and were seen in many funeral directors' premises until the 1950s. (*F.W. Paine collection*)

The interior of the former head office at 24 London Road, Kingston. The premises extend back to Fairfield North. The original wood panelling and glass remain unaltered throughout. The entrance from Fairfield is no longer in use. (*Author's collection*)

A number of classical pieces of sculpture, including this one of Eve, were in the showroom at Fairfield. It is doubtful whether its intended destination was a cemetery. (*F.W. Paine collection*)

Masons in the workshop at Fairfield. The staff are Bill Turnham, Ted Kemp, Jim Gale, Bill Barrett and Steve Stevens. (*F.W. Paine collection*)

Various ledger memorials in granite and marble with the angel in the background.

This splendid angel occupied a central position in the window of the masonry showroom at Fairfield West for many years. (*Both photographs F.W. Paine collection*)

Two Doric columns form an impressive entrance to F.W. Paine's chapel of rest in the centre of the masonry works at Fairfield West, Kingston. (*F.W. Paine collection*)

The museum at Horace Road was opened in 1984 as part of the F.W. Paine centenary celebrations. The items on display not only record how F.W. Paine operated as a business, but also how funerals have changed. In one cabinet are miniature wooden coffins used to display the range available and printing blocks used for advertisements and literature. Mounted on the walls are a number of hatchments, wands, a display of handles and fittings and photographs of former branches. The table came from the old boardroom. (*Author's collection*)

When the Fairfield West site was demolished in the 1960s the head office moved to Horace Road. This service chapel was part of the original layout. (*F.W. Paine collection*)

Two views of the chapel of rest at the Raynes Park branch probably in the 1920s. The layout permitted a service to be carried out with the coffin resting in the furthest chapel area. A harmonium was provided to accompany hymn singing. (*F.W. Paine collection*)

BIBLIOGRAPHY

Albery, N. (ed.) *The Natural Death Handbook*, 3rd edn (Rider/The Natural Death Centre, 2000)

Bland, O. *The Royal Way of Death* (London, Constable, 2000)

Cannadine, D 'War and Death, Grief and Mourning in Modern Britain' in Whaley J. (ed.) *Mirrors of Mortality* (Europa, 1981)

Charter for the Bereaved, The (The Institute of Burial and Cremation Administration Inc, 1996)

Clarke, J.M. *The Brookwood Necropolis Railway*, 3rd edition (Oxford, The Oakwood Press, 1995)

Curl, J.S. *The Victorian Celebration of Death* (Sutton Publishing, 2000)

Dead Citizens' Charter, The: Document for Consultation (The National Funerals College, 1996)

Fletcher, G. *The London Nobody Knows* (Penguin, 1962)

Gavaghan, M. *The Story of the Unknown Warrior 11th November 1920* 2nd edn (M&L Publications, 1997)

Gittings, C. *Death, Burial and the Individual in Early Modern England* (Routledge, 1984)

Gorer, G. 'The Pornography of Death', in *Death, Grief and Mourning in Contemporary Britain* (The Cresset Press, 1965)

Jones, B. *Design for Death* (London, Andre Deutsch, 1967)

Jupp, P.C. *From Dust To Ashes: The Replacement of Burial by Cremation in England 1840–1967* The Congregational Lecture 1990 (The Congregational Memorial Hall Trust, 1990)

Jupp, P.C. and Gittings, C. *Death in England: An Illustrated History* (Manchester University Press, 1999)

Kerrigan, M. *Who Lies Where: A Guide to Famous Graves*, (London, Fourth Estate, 1995)

Litten, J.W.S. *The English Way of Death: The Common Funeral Since 1450* (Hale, 1991)

May, T. *The Victorian Undertaker* (Princes Risborough, Shire, 1996)

Meller, H. *London Cemeteries: An illustrated Guide and Gazetteer*, 3rd edn (Ashgate, 1999)

Puckle, B.S. *Funeral Customs: Their Origin and Development* (London, Werner Laurie, 1926)

Taylor, L. *Mourning Dress: A Costume and Social History* (George Allen & Unwin, 1983)

Walter, T. *Funerals and How to Improve Them* (Hodder and Stoughton, 1990)